LIVING IN PORTUGAL

Your Guide To The Good Life In The Old World

By **KAT KALASHIAN**

with the Editors of Live And Invest Overseas

Published by Lahardan Books

Acknowledgements

This book was so much fun to put together, and wouldn't have been possible without the help from many Portuguese and expat friends, each of whom I'm immensely grateful to—both for the tips they contributed and the fun I've had knowing them over the years and experiencing some of the things in this book with them.

First though, I'd like to thank my intrepid mother, Kathleen Peddicord, for giving me all the opportunities I've had in life, most notably, in this context, spending time in and being able to write about Portugal. I wouldn't be where I am or having half so much fun in my vocation if not for her audaciously founding Live and Invest Overseas back in the day.

Thanks to my husband, Harry, who uncomplainingly stays home with our kids when I'm off traveling, scouting, and writing on location. And thanks to my girls, who have given me such a new perspective on life and work.

Cátia Lima, a blogger and ghostwriter based in Sintra and forever in love with Portugal, deserves a round of applause for her many and varied contributions to this book. Back in 2013, she grew tired of tourists talking only about Lisbon, Porto, and the Algarve. That motivated her to start a blog, Beyond Lisbon. Check out her blog for more insider's tips into Portuguese culture. She is a wealth of information on food, local festivals, and so much more.

Joch and Jeff Woodruff, happily married for 10 years, live in the northwestern *freguesia* of Matosinhos, called Perafita—a quiet, coastal suburb of Porto. Their condo is just two-and-a-half blocks from the ocean, which allows Joch's heart to sigh at least once a day. They have been wonderful friends over the years and give so much insight to living in Northern Portugal, where few expats tend to settle.

Stephen Powell, a British journalist who worked 27 years for Reuters, has lived in the Algarve since the end of 2019. In late 2018 and early 2019 he walked the length of Portugal, covering nearly 1,500 kms (932 miles) on foot. The country won his heart and he moved from his native Wales to the Algarve. He has published two travel books, "Walking Europe's Edge, Reflections on Portugal" and "The First Toast is to Peace, Travels in the South Caucasus." He is the expert on all things walking, hiking, and birdwatching in Portugal and has some of the best stories and most specific suggestions.

Evanne Schmarder, Publisher of *Relish Portugal*, the award-winning English language food and culture magazine for Portugal lovers everywhere, was instrumental in many of the food- and recipe-related entries.

Allison Baxley is a wife to her high school sweetheart, mother of two young children, former advertising creative director, and creator of the blog Renovating Life. She and her family uprooted their comfy lives in Brooklyn in 2021 in order to start fresh in Cascais, Portugal. After living the rat race that is NYC for 11 years, they decided they wanted to slow down, enjoy more of what life and the world have to offer, and live life with more intention. Allison is a great resource for those closer to middle age with kids who are thinking of spending time in Portugal.

Alyson Sheldrake is an accomplished artist working alongside her husband, Dave, who works as a professional photographer. They moved to live full time in the Algarve in 2011, having previously holidayed there for many years. She has written three books in her "Algarve Dream Series" that are full of useful advice, enjoyable adventures, and hilarious accounts of their Algarve life in the sun. Her books are all available to purchase on Amazon.

And finally, thank you to every adventurous traveler or expat who picks this book and finds something fun or useful in its pages.

Happy trails!

Table of Contents

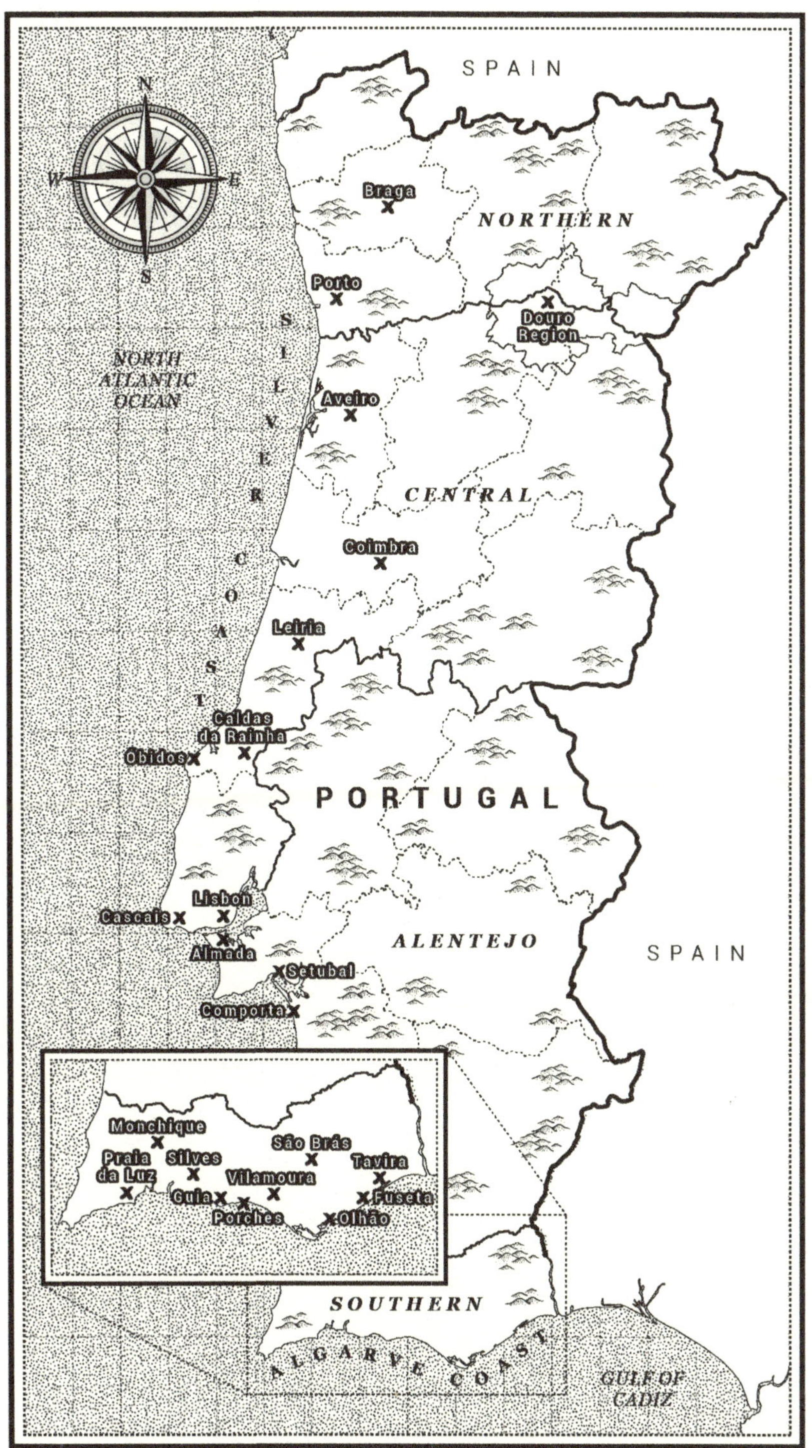

N
W
E
S
SPAIN
NORTHERN
Braga
Porto
Douro
Region
NORTH
ATLANTIC
OCEAN
SILVER COAST
Aveiro
CENTRAL
Coimbra
Leiria
Caldas
da Rainha
Óbidos
PORTUGAL
Lisbon
Cascais
Almada
Setubal
Comporta
ALENTEJO
SPAIN
Monchique
São Brás
Praia
da Luz
Silves
Vilamoura
Tavira
Guia
Fuseta
Porches
Olhão
SOUTHERN
ALGARVE COAST
GULF OF
CADIZ

Why Life In Portugal Is
As Good As Life Gets

Just what is it about Portugal that makes it so hard to resist…?

As you probably know, we named thin-sliced corners of this beautiful, sunny, friendly, safe, welcoming, and affordable country as the world's top retirement haven for nine years running.

What is it, exactly, about Portugal that makes it so tough to beat when considering options the whole globe over for places to spend time—and perhaps even reinvent your life?

In fact, Portugal checks every box on the potential explorer, expat, or investor's list…

1. **Great weather.** This region enjoys one of the most stable climates in the world with 3,300 hours of sunshine per year in the south, meaning more sunny days than almost anywhere else in Europe. The north gets less sunshine and more rain, but the climate is temperate year-round, never getting extremely hot or cold.

   The southern coast, known as the Algarve, has a long-standing reputation as a top summer destination among European sun-seekers and a top winter retreat for those looking to escape Northern Europe's coldest months. The Algarve has no bad weather months, but it does have a winter. January and February can be cold enough that you'll want a coat. The best months can be September and October, when the summer crowds have gone but the weather and sea temperature are still ideal.

2. **Safety.** Portugal ranked as the 7th safest country in the world for 2024 and has consistently been ranked as one of the most peaceful countries in the world, ranking in the top 10, if not the top 5, for over a decade now.

    Violent crime is rare, and petty crime is limited to street crime during the busy tourist season. As well, this country has managed to keep itself separate from the immigration crisis that is playing out in other parts of Europe.

3. **Good infrastructure.** Portugal has enjoyed important infrastructure investments in recent years, specifically to do with the country's highway network and airports. As a result, this is an easy region to get around and also a great base for exploring all of Europe and North Africa.

4. **International-standard health care available for a very low cost.** As a result, medical tourism is a growing industry here, in particular for cosmetic, hip replacement, and dental specialties.

5. **Golf.** Portugal is recognized as a top golfing destination in continental Europe and the world, with 77 clubs and 102 courses registered in 2024. In 2023 and 2024 it was named Best Golf Destination in the World at the World Golf Awards.

    The Algarve alone boasts 42 courses in less than 100 miles, and its year-round sunshine mean it's always pleasant to spend time outdoors.

    - ❖ Best Sustainable Water Capture System (Santo da Serra Golf Club, Madeira)
    - ❖ Best Emerging Golf Destination in the World (Madeira)
    - ❖ Best Golf Course (Terras da Comporta)
    - ❖ Best Par 3 Hole (Santo da Serra Golf Club, Madeira)
    - ❖ Best Panoramic Golf Club (Palheiro Golf, Madeira)

6. **Great beaches.** The Algarve's 100 miles of Atlantic coastline are punctuated by jagged rock formations, lagoons, and extensive

sandy beaches, with hundreds claiming coveted Blue Flags from the European Blue Flag Association, which ranks beaches based on environmental, educational, safety, and accessibility factors. In 2024, 404 beaches and marinas were awarded blue flags.

The water off these shores is azure, and the cliff-top vistas are spectacular. Most beaches have lifeguards during the summer season. Note that restaurants and snack bars are sometimes open only seasonally.

7. **Affordable cost of living.** The cost of living in Portugal is among the lowest in Western Europe, on average 30% lower than in any other country of the region.

   A couple could live here comfortably but modestly on a budget of as little as 1,300 euros per month. With a budget of 2,000 euros per month or more, you could enjoy a fully appointed lifestyle in this heart of the Old World.

8. **For the reasons described above, English is widely spoken.** Living here, you could get by without learning to speak Portuguese... though any effort to learn the local language is a show of respect and appreciated.

9. **Healthy living.** The Portuguese are the biggest fish eaters per capita in Europe, and fresh fish of great variety is available in the ever-present daily markets. The abundance of sunshine in this part of the world means an abundance of fresh produce, too, also available in the local markets. Meantime, pollution rates are low, and streets, towns, and beaches are kept clean and litter-free.

10. **One of the most user-friendly residency options in the Eurozone.** If you'd like to live in the country full time you can arrange to do so simply by showing a reliable income of at least 1,200 euros per month. Many countries offer similar residency programs based on guaranteed income; however, these are typically targeting foreign retirees and come with age restrictions.

That is not the case in Portugal. Anyone of any age who can prove income to meet the requirement can be granted the right to remain in Portugal long term. This is one of the easiest residency hurdles of any country in Europe. Indeed, it's one of the easiest of any country in the world.

Kat Kalashian
Editorial Director, Europe Division
Live and Invest Overseas

P.S. *The best way, of course, to find out if Portugal could be the ideal place for you to reinvent your life is to come see it for yourself.*

And now, at last, you can… with our help.

Our Live And Invest In Portugal Conference takes place every April and is your chance to put your boots on the ground in this beautiful sun-drenched corner of the Old World.

Attendees meet dozens of our most trusted friends and Portuguese advisors, as well as expats and fellow readers interested in a life in Portugal.

We've been hosting this event for over 10 years now, and it's the only event of its kind in the world, introducing you to a wide network of professionals while also providing you real insights on living and investing in Portugal.

Find out more at LiveandInvestOverseas.com.

The Best Of Portugal
For The Traveler

1. Eating, Drinking, And Special Stays

For many, cuisine, café culture, and the pleasures of long, wine-filled meal are a big part of the attraction of life in Portugal. And eating your way across the country is not a bad way to get to know the local culture.

Not to mention the coffee that's taken so seriously, the delicious wine that no good gourmand could live without, the fresh-from-the-net seafood that's available year-round, or the indulgent sweet treats that are so close to the heart of every Portuguese.

When it comes to living in Portugal, your tastebuds play a big role in enjoying the local traditions…

Northern Portugal

⊚ Aveiro

The real eel: Aveiro's legendary caldeirada

Aveiro is the best place to get eel in Portugal. The most traditional way to have it is in a *caldeirada*, a fish and/or seafood stew made in either a *cataplana* or a Dutch oven. Here it's famous for being made with eels, and it's the only region to do so. The recipe was created to use up the leftovers from fishermen's catches and became emblematic of the region.

A Tasca do Confrade offers an impeccable traditional *caldeirada de enguias*, eel stew, which is a specialty of Aveiro. The stew is seasoned with saffron and best accompanied with a Bairrada white wine.

Make sure to try the fried eels as a starter. If you manage to also try eel with *escabeche* sauce, you'll have sampled the trifecta of eel dishes.

***

Eggstacy in Aveiro

Ovos moles de Aveiro is sweet cream made of egg yolks and sugar, usually sold in a wafer-like shell but also used as filling or topping for cakes and pastries. Not to be missed if you're in a local bakery.

***

⊚ **Braga**

Portugal's best-kept duck secret

Although Portugal is not famous for duck, the classic *arroz de pato* dish is a specialty, especially in Braga. It can be a bit greasy, but *arroz de pato* (duck rice) is one of the most filling and simple dishes on any menu.

A bit like a risotto, the secret is in the broth, used first to cook the duck, then the rice. Add slices of chorizo, and you have a hearty meal, great in the winter. This Portuguese comfort food is a perfect Sunday dinner. It uses Agulha rice, a long grain variety that remains long with separate distinguishable grains when cooked.

***

⊚ **Costa Verde** (also known as the Minho Region)

Stirring up the soul: the soup-er iconic broth that built a nation

This region, formerly known as the Minho region, is said to be the homeplace of what is perhaps Portugal's most beloved comfort food: *caldo verde*. It's seen as the unofficial dish of Portugal, and you'll find it everywhere. It's cheap, tasty, and filling. Pair it with the rustic country cornbread, *broa*, and you'll understand why this simple soup is so iconic.

Ask any Portuguese person, and they're sure to tell you that the most iconic dish of their country is *caldo verde* (literally, green broth). It gets its name from the thinly sliced greens that are mixed in with water or stock, along with potato, garlic, onion, and sausage, which creates a dish that's more of a meal than a soup.

A simple recipe, it's not really green, and it's not really a broth... Instead, it's a blended mix of onion, garlic, potatoes, and olive oil. Some recipes include *chouriço* or even smoky *salpicão* (sausage). But the star ingredient is the greens: *couve galega* (Galician cabbage), a type of leafy kale.

The trick? It must be finely shredded. You'll find this healthy green fresh at any market, but it's also available pre-sliced in the bagged greens section of any grocery.

You'll see this dish on menus across the country, but if you want to taste how it's made on its own turf, you've got to have it in the Costa Verde region.

***

The golden bread of the north: a slice of Portuguese history

The local cornbread, *broa de milho*, is a staple of this northern region. Made with yellow corn flour, salt, and sourdough or baker's yeast, this is probably the most common type of *broa* (there are many) and the reason why most Portuguese associate this bread with the color yellow.

Broa in general is a traditional type of bread that holds cultural significance—it has been a staple food for centuries, especially in rural areas. It uses a mix of wheat, corn, and rye flour, which gives it a unique taste, texture, versatility, and slightly sweet and tangy flavor.

(Note that there's a sort of small cake, round or oval shaped, that is also called a *broa*. These are sweet but dense and heavy. It's easy to tell the difference: if they're small, they're the sweet kind.)

Today, *broa* is seen as a hearty, rustic bread that has an irreplaceable spot in certain occasions and circumstances, having more "character" than regular wheat bread.

Historically, this type of bread was more commonly found in North and Central Portugal, where corn and rye were easier to grow than wheat. This also made *broa* the bread of the poor. Today, it's still closely associated with those regions, but you can find it virtually everywhere in good supermarkets and bakeries.

It's often used for sandwiches (with regional types of cheese and *presunto* or other cured meats) or as a side for soups and snacks, like flame-grilled *chouriço*. When it comes to soup, the quintessential Portuguese pairing is a slice of *broa* with a bowl of piping hot *caldo verde* (see above).

Another common pairing, especially during the summer months, is eating small grilled fish (like sardines) with a slice of *broa* underneath. The bread soaks up the fat and flavor from the fish.

The more sophisticated uses include cheese and cured meat boards, as well as a dish called *bacalhau com broa*, where a thick cod loin is covered in crumbled up *broa*.

As with *caldo verde*, you'll see this outside of this northern region… but if you get up this far north, you'd be doing yourself a disservice to not try it in its place of origin.

***

Go hog wild on Bairrada's juiciest secret

The Bairrada region is one of two places in the country known for a dish that isn't often featured on tourist routes: roasted suckling pig (*leitão assado*, here known as *Leitão da Bairrada*).

Here, the dish is made with a Bísara breed of pig which must be between 8 and 10 kgs, its diet strictly milk and some regulated farm scavenging, mostly on acorns. The pig must then be roasted in a wood-burning oven using vine firewood, often the same vines to give the Baga grapes used to make the local wines.

After a couple of hours, the final product should be crispy on the outside and juicy on the inside. If all these criteria are fulfilled, the pork will meet the IGP (Protected Geographical Indication) certification standard—which is to say, it's official.

Plus, it pairs perfectly with the local Espumante da Bairrada wine.

Mealhada, a small town in the region, is the roasted pig mecca of the country. Located on the highway between Lisbon and Porto which was a much-used supply route, back in 1943 Álvaro Pedro realized there was a good business to be made in feeding the passing truckers—even something as simple as a pork sandwich—and opened the restaurant that started it all. Within a few years, he was successful enough to open Pedro Dos Leitões. Family run to this day, the restaurant can feed over 400 people per sitting and send out 100+ pigs a day. Rival restaurants soon followed Pedro's example, and Mealhada's reputation as hog heaven was immortalized. Today, you'll see local families pour into this little town each weekend for a pig lunch.

***

Pork, blood, and glory: from medieval to mouthwatering

The not-for-the-faint of heart *arroz de serrabulho* (which translates to "pig blood rice") is a rice dish featuring both pork meat and blood—both in liquid and sausage form—along with cumin, nutmeg, and cloves. It may also include beef and/or chicken.

The origins of this dish—that induces so much dread in foreigners—date back to post-Black Death Middle Ages when food was so scarce that most couldn't afford meat but could usually get their hands on some animal blood. They'd mix it with bread or other things to lend plain foods meatiness and some protein. The result was so tasty, it has endured as a signature dish of the Minho region.

Sarrabulho is served in two parts: First is the *arroz de sarrabulho*, the rice cooked in pigs' blood and chunks of blood sausage and other meats. Once cooked, most of the meat is removed and the dish is served in a bowl, almost like a risotto.

Next comes *papas de sarrabulho*, the chunks of the cooked meat that was removed (which could include pork, chicken, beef, sausage, and blood sausage) served with potatoes.

It's quite the hearty one-two punch…

And it's traditional, which is to say, essential, to pair the dish with some red vinho verde, which is served in a teacup instead of a glass.

This rich dish is so treasured that in 2006, the *Sarrabulho* Rice Brotherhood was created in the little town of Ponte de Lima (the oldest *vila* in the country) as a way of promoting and highlighting the gastronomic and historical value of this dish.

Near Ponte de Lima, Restaurant Rotunda da Feitosa has to be the best place to try this iconic dish. No foreigner is likely to come across this little spot on their own, you'd need to know about it, located as it is on a roundabout leaving town.

✳✳✳

Fizzical attraction to Portugal's sparkling secret

Sparkling fresh vinho verde hails from the Minho region (Costa Verde), so this is the place to enjoy it where it's grown and bottled. This type of wine is unique in the world and an excellent reason to explore the region. In fact, the name of the wine may refer to the greenery of the region… or could refer to the acidity that usually comes when grapes were harvested green.

Vinho verde is not a grape variety, it is a protected region for production. Literally, it means "green wine," but is more accurately translated as "young wine." The yearly production is released three to six months after the grapes, which can be of any color, are harvested. These aren't bottles to keep for aging, they are best drunk soon after bottling.

Usually sparkling, vinho verde could also be a dessert wine or even brandy. In its infancy, the typical effervesce came from natural fermentation, which was traditionally considered a fault. However, producers in Portugal found that consumers liked the slight fizz. Today, most producers simply add a slight sparkle by artificial carbonation.

The white, the most well-known and best-loved, is an aromatic and refreshing drink, enjoyed as an aperitif, with salads, snacks or just a break on a hot day. No matter the color, they are best drunk chilled and pair perfectly with seafood.

The Minho region is full of many small growers, many of whom used to train their vines high off the ground, up trees, fences, and even telephone poles so that they could cultivate vegetable crops below the vines. Head to this region to visit one—or several!—for a tour or tasting.

***

Brûlée the Portuguese way

For traditional northern desserts, the Costa Verde (also known as the Minho region) is famous for its *leite creme*, a rich version of *crème brûlée*, infused with lemon and cinnamon—not to be missed.

***

Souperiority complex: Viana's version or nothing

While the southern Algarve region is often famed for its fish dishes, no one ever talks about seafood traditions in the north…

In the farthest northern coastal tip of the country, a little town called Viana do Castelo in the Costa Verde region makes a distinctive fish soup called *chorinha*, which includes tomatoes, peppers, and fresh coriander.

If you make it this far north, you need to try this variation on the basic dish, which, when made elsewhere, is often called "in the style of Viana." But of course, if you don't have it in Viana, it can't be the real thing…

***

⊚ Porto

Belle Époque, big dreams: the most beautiful café in Porto

Café Majestic is a stunningly ornate café that opened its doors in 1922 and retains its original, over-the-top luxury aesthetic throughout. Going through its doors is like stepping back in time…back to when writers and artists gathered here for their intellectual debates, when musicians came to write lyrics, and poets came to contemplate life. Its history tells the story of the city…

Perhaps the most emblematic café in Porto, Café Majestic has hosted many prominent figures over the years and is considered to be one of the most beautiful cafés in the world. The emblematic Belle Époque architecture and luxurious interior make it a popular destination for locals and tourists alike—and no trip to Porto would be complete without a visit here… perhaps for their famous 5 O'clock Tea…

Brews And Brains, Percolating Ideas
Since the 18th Century

Cafés in Portugal have a rich history, and some of the oldest cafés in Lisbon and Porto have been operating since the 18th and 19th centuries. Their walls witnessed important cultural and political events, and were where many a famous poet or scholar penned their works. They were a second home for Portuguese intellectuals, artists, and writers over the centuries…

***

Sippin' and swingin': Porto's café for culture and chords

Café Guarany has been serving customers in its elegant art deco style since 1933. The café's ambience is dedicated to Southern American natives who once dominated the vast region that today is home to Paraguay, Paraná (Brazil), and Uruguay. It is a cultural landmark in the city, attracting artists, writers, and musicians throughout the years. Fridays and Saturdays are dedicated to live music—Cuban and fado. When enjoying the music here, don't forget to appreciate two paintings by Graça Morais "The Lords of Amazonia," depicting the Guarany tribe.

***

Guts and glory: Porto's proudest plate

Tripe is a historically beloved ingredient in Porto whose popularity dates back to the 1415 expedition of Prince Henry the Navigator, when sailors preparing for their journey were given all the good cuts of meat. Left with entrails, the people of Porto, called *tripeiros*, after their story of tripe, made do.

If life gives you tripe, you use it to create a new dish—one that is still enjoyed today: *tripas à moda do Porto*. A hearty stew with tripe, vegetables, and white beans, it rules supreme in the hearts of many Portuguese, especially those from Porto.

***

Decoded: A Shot-By-Shot Guide To Ordering Coffee Like a Local

When it comes to coffee in Portugal, espresso is the drink of choice. Commonly referred to simply as café, some people will also call it *bica* (when in Lisbon) or *cimbalino* (when in Porto). You'll often get a cinnamon stick in substitution for or alongside a spoon.

When you order, you are likely to be asked if you want it light or dark (weaker or stronger) and the coffee-to-milk ratio will be adjusted accordingly. In cities and bigger towns you might find vegetable milk options, but it's not typical in smaller areas.

Here's a guide to the types of coffee drink you'll find here...

- ❖ ***Café cheio*** - A normal espresso to which more hot water is added; also served in an espresso cup.
- ❖ ***Café curto*** - A smaller espresso.
- ❖ ***Descafeinado*** - Decaf.
- ❖ ***Garoto*** - An espresso to which warm milk is added almost to the brim of the cup. In the north of Portugal, this is often called a *pingo* or *café pingado*.
- ❖ ***Galão*** - A glass with an espresso filled up with warm milk.
- ❖ ***Meia de leite*** - A cup (slightly bigger than a tea cup) with an espresso and filled up with warm milk.
- ❖ ***Abatanado* or americano** - One espresso to which they add enough hot water to fill the cup (the same size cup that's used for *meia de leite*).
- ❖ ***Carioca de limão*** - Lemon peel in hot water. It can be served in an espresso cup or in the *meia de leite* cup.
- ❖ ***Café com cheirinho*** - An espresso with added aguardente (similar to brandy). Drunk after lunch, this is not the kind of thing you're likely to find in touristy places.

✳✳✳

The bread that built a town, rising since 1563

Broa de Avintes is the local type of peasant bread, made with a mix of corn and rye flour and sourdough and baked for several hours. This bread made in Avintes, a town near Porto, is a dark and dense *broa* with a flour-covered surface. The first written reference to it, that we know of, dates back to 1563. Since 1989, the town has even organized a yearly festival dedicated to its special *broa*.

✳✳✳

Saucy, stacked, and slightly sinful: The original little French girl

Loosely based on the French croque monsieur, which is basically a grilled cheese with ham in the middle, the *francesinha* (literally, "little French girl") is a 20th-century creation and the signature sandwich of Porto—it is not for the weak or faint-hearted.

Two thick slices of bread are stuffed with as much and as many kinds of meat as they can fit—usually steak, ham, sausage, or chorizo—then coated in melted cheese and a spicy tomato and beer sauce…

Need an extra few calories? Add a fried egg on top for good measure. Too much? Wait until you realize it comes with a side of fries.

This sandwich is found all over the country, in fact, these days it's so popular there are even vegetarian and vegan versions. But if you want the real deal, make sure to get one in Porto.

***

Portugal's liquid legacy: aged to perfection, fortified with flair

Portugal has been producing fortified port wines for over 250 years. They are made from a blend of several grapes that are grown in the Douro Valley near Porto.

Port is made by adding a distilled grape spirit, usually brandy, to a wine base. The addition of the high-alcohol spirit stabilizes the wine, stops fermentation, and fortifies the wine. This process gives it a punch of around 20% alcohol by volume.

***

Vines and vessels, sail and swirl: reds, whites and river delights

A cruise on the Douro River, which lets out into the Atlantic at Porto, is perhaps the most unique way to experience wine country… A Douro wine cruise is one of the most unique and rewarding ways to experience this region. The birthplace of Port wine, one of the world's most iconic fortified wines, this region also produces high-quality red and whites.

Many cruises include exclusive access to wine estates (*quintas*) for tastings and tours.

Central Portugal

⦿ Beira

Tentacle temptations: Portugal's perfect octopus plate

Polvo à lagareiro (octopus with olive oil and potatoes) is said to have originated in the central Portuguese region known as the Beiras. Octopus, tentacles and all, is boiled then soaked in olive oil and garlic and roasted. It's served alongside boiled or baked potatoes that are mashed, salted, and tossed in olive oil with coriander or other herbs.

***

From apothecary to aperitif

Licor Beirão originated in the 19th century and is the most consumed spirit in Portugal.

The liquor is made from a double distillation of seeds and herbs from all over the world, many brought to Portugal from its former colonies of Brazil, Sri Lanka, and India. The recipe includes mint and lavender, which are grown on the family estate, plus cinnamon and cardamom.

It was originally created by a pharmacy in Lousã as a medicinal product for stomach aches. By the end of the 19th century, alcohols were no longer qualified as medicinal, but the son-in-law of the original producer kept making it.

In 1929 it was entered into a contest where it earned a gold medal and its name of Beirão.

***

⦿ Caldas da Rainha

Lunch like a local, pay like a peasant

For a typical Portuguese *menu do dia* (daily menu), head over to "O

Telheirinho," right in front of the Dom Carlos I Park, where you can get the daily special with a main dish, drink, and espresso for a little under 10 euros.

* * *

Daily Deals, Delicious Dishes:
The *Menu Do Dia* Explained

Restaurants across Portugal announce their *menu do dia*, or daily menu. Whether you're in the north or the south, in a city or a village—you're bound to come across a menu of the day.

...But what exactly is it?

A *menu do dia* is a fixed-price lunch menu of several courses. It can vary from restaurant to restaurant, but typically consists of a starter, a main course, and a dessert or a drink (or an espresso).

These often cater to a mostly fixed clientele, so eateries choose their main dishes based on what their regulars prefer—especially true in office-heavy neighborhoods.

And dishes are highly seasonal. In spring, for example, as soon as fava beans appear on the markets, you can expect to see them on daily menus as well. In June, it's hard not to see one that includes grilled sardines or mackerel.

Going for a *menu do dia* means having a good, cheap, and balanced meal delivered quickly and at a modest price. More often than not, it's also an amazing opportunity to experience authentic local flavors.

Starter: Usually a soup, often a vegetable soup, sometimes with bread. You might also see a salad offered from time to time.

Main Course: Usually a choice of meat or fish (chicken, pork, cod, or salmon) with a side of rice, potatoes (sometimes both), or salad. Vegetarian options are more common in urban areas. A side salad is very basic because the Portuguese tend to eat the majority of their veggies in the form of soup.

Dessert: If included, likely either a traditional Portuguese des-

sert (*leite creme, pudim, arroz doce*, or *maçã assada*), or fruit.
   Beverage: Bottle of water, carafe of house wine, or a soft drink.
   Prices: Depends on the food offered as well as location and type of restaurant, but expect to pay 10 euros on average. In touristy areas or upscale restaurants, 15 to 20 euros is more likely.

***

Haute cuisine, low-key prices

For those in the mood for something upscale but with great value for money "O Tacho" is well worth the detour in Caldas da Rainha.

***

Cool Sips in shady spots

"Cais do Parque," right in the Dom Carlos I Park, has seats outside, serves meals, and is also a wonderful option for a coffee or a cold drink.

***

⦿ Cascais

Seafood and sea views

On the bay from Cascais, a few restaurants of note sit side by side and offer spectacular views over Cascais Bay—"Hífen" and "Baía de Peixe." The former serves modern versions of Portuguese classics, and the latter serves up a feast of seafood dishes at reasonable prices.

***

Herbivore heaven in Cascais

There are a few restaurants that offer veggie-forward menus in Cascais: "Fauna and Flora" near the São Pedro do Estoril train station, "Tete's

Burritos," "House of Wonders" and "Tanah Vegan" in Cascais center to name a few.

****

Top spot for true tascas *vibes*

The Cascais marina area has many wonderful dining spots to consider, as well as beautiful views of the marina and Citadel. In general, these locations offer more authenticity than some of the more tourist-focused dining options in the center and along the Paredão.

****

⊚ **Coimbra**

Custard and chords in a cloister

Café Santa Cruz is housed in a former church that dates back to the 12th century and is part of the Santa Cruz Monastery, which is next door. It was transformed into a café in 1923 and has since been a meeting place for students, locals, and visitors.

Besides being a nice spot for a pastry and a coffee, they also have free fado de Coimbra shows at 6 p.m. and 10 p.m. fado de Coimbra is different from the most well-known Lisbon fado in several aspects, but most notably for the fact that it is sung only by men, typically either students or former students of the university.

While you're here, why not try a local pastry? Perhaps the Pastel de Tentúgal, a sort of roll made with an incredibly light, flaky dough and filled with egg cream created by a local Carmelite nun. Or the *crúzio*, a pastry shell filled with egg cream and topped with almond slivers that was crafted by the café in the mid-20th century. When in doubt, try both!

****

Coimbra's classiest clink with a view

Head over to Rua Estrela in Coimbra to find a bar and restaurant called "Passaporte." This is a great spot for a cocktail or snacks. Added bonus: the magnificent view over the city and the river.

****

A Shot of Espresso, a Slice of Life:
The Portuguese Café Way

A Portuguese café is so much more than a place for a coffee or snack—it's a vibrant social hub, a coworking space, and a meeting place all mixed into one…

For many in Portugal, the café is a second home, a modern version of the village square where people would meet in days of old.

As much as locals love coffee (espresso, in most cases), the setting itself is key. Coffee is important, but *the café* is vital.

Today, cafés are an institution in Portuguese society.

Friends of all ages gather in cafés, be they teenager or retiree. In urban areas, they're also coworking spaces, and they often serve as the backdrop for first dates. Some offer free newspapers and magazines for patrons to read and share.

There are a few categories of café you might see:

* *Pastelarias* are pastry shops; even better is a *pastelaria com fabrico próprio*, which makes its own cakes, pastries, and savory items.
* *Cantinho do café*, or coffee corner, often found in metro or train stations, with a small selection of snacks.
* If it's a snack bar, then you've found yourself a café that also serves basic meals, but don't expect anything too complex or fancy.

Especially in cities, it's common for commuters to stop by a café after breakfast for a quick coffee and maybe a pastry before work.

Mid-morning and mid-afternoon will also see folks rushing in for a caffeine boost.

Lunch break? The perfect time for coworkers to socialize over an espresso.

Around 5 p.m., particularly in the suburbs and smaller towns, you'll see kids and their grandparents going to the café for an after-school snack, as well as teenagers sharing treats with friends.

Ordering an espresso and sitting there for a good while just people-watching is not uncommon and is not frowned upon— unless it's a busy time of the day or you're in a touristy area.

People with laptops, working, or studying? Also a fairly common sight, although mostly in the cities, and, again, not something that is usually frowned upon.

A special note on café staff: if you're a regular, there's a good chance you'll be treated like family after a while.

They'll remember if you prefer your toast with lots of butter, and if you look sleepy, they'll ask if you want your coffee drink darker (meaning, with more coffee), because they already know you'll probably say yes.

History's tastiest retirement plan (for goats)

Just outside of Coimbra, two little towns make a bold claim. Vila Nova de Poiares and Miranda do Corvo both call themselves the Capital of *Chanfana*. This goat stew is specifically made from the meat of a very aged goat—those no longer producing milk or kids. It's noted in writings going back to the 17th century by the likes of Miguel de Cervantes, Bocage, Nicholas Tolentino, and Miguel Torga.

Although the meal is traditionally the ultimate peasant dish (the reason for using old goat), nowadays it's often made with lamb or kid. Though these new versions are available throughout the country, for the original version, head to either Vila Nova de Poiares and Miranda do Corvo and find a rustic local place.

A proper *chanfana* should be prepared a day in advance, the meat well marinaded in a robust concoction of much red wine, bay leaf, garlic, and olive oil. Roasted in traditional black clay pots inside of wood-fired ovens (or, more likely these days, an ordinary kitchen oven), the stew should simmer for at least a couple of hours.

***

The gayest good time for miles

Angel's Bar is a well-known gay-friendly bar in town, and about an hour to the south, in Leiria, Glitz Club is another queer favorite.

***

Tentúgal's tastiest national treasure

In Coimbra, rectangular-shaped pastries known as pastéis de Tentúgal (the name of a village near Coimbra) are popular. These traditional sweets, filled with an egg yolk and almond cream and wrapped in a thin, crumbly dough, will satisfy your sweet tooth.

***

The most personalized bread in Portugal

The local type of bread, *broa de Loriga*, which comes from Loriga, a town in the Serra da Estrela region, is made with white corn flour, salt, and sourdough or baker's yeast. The shape is round and slightly flat. The interior is dry, porous, and off-white.

Being deeply rooted in local history, this *broa* was consumed almost exclusively for more than two centuries. The bread for home consumption by most families was cooked in community ovens, managed by bakers who organized the entire task of baking the bread. The breads were identified with "pinches" or holes to know who they belonged to.

***

⊚ Évora

The other kind of queijada

This little town in the middle of the country offers its own twist on Sintra's famous *queijada*. Another national *queijada* celebrity, this one is made with sheep's milk cheese.

⊚ Leiria

The wonder dish that puts paella to shame

Leiria's has the honor of being the home town of one of Portugal's most typical dishes: *arroz de marisco* (seafood rice), which you could think of as a local seafood version of paella. It's such an iconic dish that it was named one of the 7 Wonders of Portuguese Gastronomy.

The Leirian way of serving the meal is in a clay pot, which is filled with shrimp, clams, crab, lobster, mussels, and cockles, and anything else that's in the market that day, along with the rice.

***

The everything stew: a potful of Portuguese soul

About 30 minutes south of Leiria is Alcobaça, home of the *frango na púcara*, or, "chicken in a pot." A kind of rich chicken stew cooked clay jug called a *púcara*, the chicken is accompanied by ham, chorizo, tomato, onion, carrot, port, brandy, mustard, garlic, bay leaf, and any number of other ingredients depending on the chef and what's on hand.

***

Old bread, new legends: Portugal's tastiest reinventions

Two of Portugal's most simple and delicious dishes are *açorda* and *migas*. You'd be forgiven for confusing the two. While *açordas* are loose, more along the lines of soup or porridge, *migas* are more cake-like.

Migas (crumbled bread or bread crumbs) is made of stale bread, usually served in the morning but not always. Garlic, olive oil, and, of course, stale bread are common ingredients, but the add-ins range from meat to vegetables depending on your taste.

Portugal offers up two regional varieties: Beiras region uses cornbread, *broa*, while in Alentejo, they use white bread.

***

Portugal's most perfectly imperfect cake

Pão de Ló de Alfeizerão, a symbol of local pride, is a wonderfully simple yet decadent dessert. Made with only three ingredients: eggs, sugar, and flour, the secret to the recipe is in the baking. Left slightly undercooked and runny in the center, it's like a custard and a cake in one.

The cake dates to the 18th century, when a nun named Amália who lived in the convent of Alfeizerão came up with the recipe. She made it for special occasions, but its popularity boomed in the town and soon those from nearby.

***

⦿ Lisbon

Java joint for the literary giants

"A Brasileira," in the heart of Lisbon, is one of the most famous cafés in Portugal. It was founded in 1905 and quickly became a meeting place for artists, intellectuals, and bohemians. The café's interior retains its original Art Nouveau style, and it is known for its iconic bronze statue of the Portuguese writer Fernando Pessoa, who was a regular customer.

***

Not A Coffee Lover?

While coffee is the staple, if you're not a coffee person, there are plenty of good options for a local specialty...

Hot chocolate is the top replacement for coffee. Ucal, a brand that has become synonymous with chocolate milk in Portugal, is found everywhere (along with some other brands).

Compal fruit juices, particularly their peach and pear flavors, are a beloved drink, and one of the reasons is that they often use local varieties of fruit, like *pêra rocha* (a native variety of pear) and oranges from the Algarve (famous for being juicy and sweet).

Soda lover? Try the Portuguese brand Sumol—it's a beloved local soda.

Alcoholic beverages are also available in most cafés, with Sagres and Super Bock being the most common beers.

***

To rival royalty

"Pastelaria Versailles" is a renowned pastry shop and café established in Lisbon in 1922 by founders who wanted to create a luxury hot spot inspired by the grandeur of Versailles in France. Expect high ceilings, crystal chandeliers, and Art Nouveau mirrors.

***

Where Lisbon's greatest minds gathered

"Café Nicola" was founded in 1787 by an Italian named Nicola and was originally called "Botequim do Nicola." Located in Rossio Square in Lisbon, it used to be a gathering place for intellectuals, politicians, and writers. Among its frequent customers was the poet Bocage and, later, the writer Eça de Queirós, the main figure in the first wave of Portuguese literary realism.

***

Mugs and manuscripts

"Café Martinho da Arcada" is located in Praça do Comércio in Lisbon The original establishment opened in 1778, but it was only in 1782 that it was officially inaugurated. Another favorite among artists, writers, and politicians, Martinho da Arcada was also among Fernando Pessoa's most cherished places (yes, the same Fernando Pessoa that also used to frequent "A Brasileira")… so much in fact that he even had a favorite table.

***

Portugal's booziest bonbon

In Portugal, sour cherries play a unique role, not for eating but for drinking. *Ginjinha* is the traditional liqueur made from sour cherries and with strong ties to Lisbon, Óbidos, and Alcobaça. *Ginjinha*, which is made from the maceration of sour cherries, is meant to be drunk at the end of meals as a digestive.

Today, you'll often find *ginjinha* served in tiny chocolate cups, especially in touristy areas. This started some years ago, during one of the editions of the Óbidos Chocolate Festival, and it was such a hit that many establishments have since adopted this new way of serving *ginja*.

Originally, however, it was served in small glasses, either plain or with a few sour cherries at the bottom of the glass. Some places still serve it this way. If you want your *ginjinha* with a few sour cherries, say "*com elas*" (meaning "with them"), but if not, then say "*sem elas*" ("without them").

If you notice a sign on a shop window saying "*Ginja* for kids," don't panic: it's only a sort of cherry-flavored light syrup served in tiny chocolate cups.

***

Cocktails in a cabinet of curiosities

"Pavilhão Chinês," a bar in the trendy Bairro Alto neighborhood, is housed in a 1901 building that was formerly a grocery store. It was originally opened as an antique store, but when the sociable owner realized he was serving drinks more than selling goods, he opened a bar inside.

The cavernous bar's five rooms are packed with curios, toys, figurines, antiques, dolls, artwork, war relics, and endless collections of innumerable tchotchkes that have taken over every surface in the place. There's also pool tables, as if you needed any more entertainment here.

The menu is a tome, and they are very reluctant to hand them out, as they are works of art in themselves. You'll be urged to use the QR code, but with a menu this big, it's hard to browse on a phone. As well as every cocktail you've ever heard of, and many more that you haven't, there are over 40 kinds of tea, dozens of liquors and alcohols of every type, every kind of juice, and some basic snacks.

This immersive oddity is served by a staff that wears old fashioned uniforms, complete with bowtie and vest. You'll need to ring the bell to get in, and you won't be allowed to go in just to wander or take photos, but once you buy something, feel free to snap away.

***

Portugal's sweetest icon

Pastéis de nata are a Portuguese classic. Other than cod, these little tarts are probably the most iconic food associated with Portugal, and are said to have originated in the Jerónimos Monastery in Lisbon.

This mini tart consists of a rich, lightly sweetened custard encased in a crisp puff pastry shell. Whether you have it for breakfast or as an afternoon snack, pastéis de nata are a cheap and cheerful indulgence. They cost a euro each, and you never need to go far to find one in Portugal.

Locals will usually add a shake of cinnamon on top and enjoy the snack with an espresso.

⊚ **Montemor-o-Velho**

Blood, wine, and eel: Coimbra's boldest bite

Coimbra is famous for *arroz de lampreia* (lamprey rice) and other eel-based dishes, which are seasonal, only prepared from January to April. These nightmarish, blood-sucking creatures are marinated in their own blood—perhaps a karmic retribution?—before being cooked in a broth of blood, wine (red vinho verde), and some flavorings, then simmered for hours until tender.

Although this dish is found across Portugal, with each region varying the recipe slightly according to local preferences, Coimbra and its environs are probably the most well known for the dish. Every March, 30,000 or so food lovers inundate the little village of Montemor-o-Velho, about 30 minutes or so from Coimbra, for the annual Lamprey and Rice Festival.

✳✳✳

⊚ **Negrais**

Central Portugal's prized piglet

Negrais, to the north of Lisbon and the Sintra municipality, is well known for its roasted suckling pig, *leitão assado*, known here as *leitão de Negrais*, and it's one of the Portuguese specialties that you don't often see on the tourist routes.

A piglet of no more than 8 kgs is spitted and roasted in a bread oven for around two hours, until the skin is oh-so-crispy and the meat is tender and juicy.

Negrais is one of two places where this dish is cherished and especially popular, the other, the Bairrada region, is found even farther north, on the road between Lisbon and Porto, near Coimbra. In Negrais, the pig is put in the oven flattened and "open," whereas in Bairrada, it's tied up before being roasted.

Make sure to pair it with a sparkling wine, particularly good with this dish is Espumante da Bairrada, from Negrais' *leitão assado* sister city.

You'll sometimes see it in restaurants in the region and in Lisbon, too, but Negrais is the home of this specialty—or at least one of them!

***

⦿ Óbidos

Burgers, brews, and castle views

If you're looking for something a bit different but still Portuguese, try "Letraria Óbidos." Located next to the outside of the castle walls, here you'll find snacks, hamburgers, and sandwiches but the real stars are the craft beers, made in the north of Portugal. The outside seating also provides some quiet in an otherwise often busy Óbidos.

⦿ Serra da Estrela

The first cheese of Portugal—and still the finest

Serra da Estrela PDO (Protected Denomination of Origin) cheese is the oldest of Portuguese cheeses, with records mentioning it as far back as the Middle Ages. This cheese is produced exclusively from the raw milk of Churra Mondegueira or Bordaleira Serra da Estrela sheep, entirely handmade by skilled cheesemakers. A key ingredient in its production is the thistle flower. Another crucial element is the temperature of the cheesemaker's hands.

It needs a minimum of 30 days to mature, resulting in a white or slightly yellowish semi-soft, buttery paste. The flavor is smooth and slightly acidic.

When matured for at least 120 days, it's called Serra da Estrela Velho (aged) cheese, distinguished by its persistent aroma and strong to slightly spicy and salty flavor. This version of the cheese has a semi-hard to extra-hard paste.

Usually shared on special occasions, like Christmas, New Year's, birthdays, or any celebration. You can also find it on the cheese and charcuterie table at weddings and christenings.

Most Portuguese enjoy Serra da Estrela on a slice of rustic country bread called *broa* (a dense rye or corn bread) or crackers.

A traditional pairing is a slice of quince paste (*marmelada*) or a spoonful of pumpkin jam with broken-up walnuts for extra crunch. Other flavors that work well are orange, honey, almond, fig, and cinnamon.

Serra da Estrela pairs well with balanced, structured wines as well as aged wines, like port or Madeira.

Many Portuguese like to cut a square "lid" on top of the cheese, remove some with a spoon, and then put the lid back on. For cheese connoisseurs, however, this is a crime equivalent to making cake batter and then eating it instead of the baked cake.

***

Portugal's cherry capital

The cherry tree was introduced to Portugal by the Romans and has made itself at home in the southeast region of central Portugal, notably in Fundão and Cova da Beira.

The Portuguese have a saying: Conversations are like cherries, with one leading to another—needless to say, these little fruits are much beloved across the country. The fact that they're only available in the summer makes them all the more coveted, and they're especially beloved in this little area where they are grown. Cherries sold elsewhere in the country proudly advertise their origin as being from this region.

***

⊙ **Setúbal**

Sip, snack, and soak in the culture

For a quick bite in Setúbal, check out the Casa da Baía Cultural Centre, which has been renovated to offer a variety of cultural experiences. This includes an indoor café, a patio, a wine shop with regional wines, temporary exhibitions, and a tourist information desk.

***

Fisherman's favorite turned regional star

The Setúbal region is known for its mouth-watering charcoal-grilled fish and seafood. Among the most popular are oysters from the Sado. The quintessential dish, however, is fried cuttlefish (*choco frito*), which started as a sort of fisherman's snack and eventually gained the status of a local specialty.

***

The pride of Azeitão

For a 100% local treat, wrap up your meal here with a sweet *torta de Azeitão* (little cake rolls filled with egg cream and powdered cinnamon) and a generous glass of Moscatel de Setúbal, a type of fortified Muscat wine.

***

⦿ Sintra

A tale of two tables in Sintra

In Sintra, try "Incomum," with an interesting mix of Portuguese and international elements, and "Apeadeiro," for a more traditional experience in a touristy part of Sintra.

Sintra's cataplana kings

"Restaurante da Adraga" and "Nortada" are among the most favored places for the traditional rice-based dishes and *cataplanas* in Sintra.

***

Tips For Portuguese Dining

You'll never be at a loss for finding incredible food in Portugal—whether local or international—and it all comes at an incredible bargain for the most part.

But in general, seek out local, family-run restaurants and don't eat in touristy areas.

Remember that it's difficult to find anywhere open to eat between 3 p.m. and 6 p.m., and things won't stay open much past 10 p.m.

***

Pig in a Portuguese blanket

At virtually any fair in the Sintra region, you'll find at least one stall selling freshly baked *pão com chouriço*, literally, bread with sausage. *Chouriço* is a type of pork and paprika smoked sausage. Smaller bakeries often make them as well.

***

The cheesecake that paid the crown

Queijo fresco, a light fresh cheese with lots of moisture and a mild flavor. It can be made from cow, goat, or sheep milk and is usually eaten with a sprinkle of salt and/or pepper. You'll often find it served as an entrée in restaurants, but the significance of this cheese goes far beyond that of being a starter: *queijo fresco* used to be so common in this area that it became the main ingredient in the local *queijadas*, essentially mini cheesecakes that Sintra has been known for for centuries.

The origin of the *queijada* is immortalized in writing that goes back at least as far as the 13th century. This little pastry used to be homemade and so coveted that they were treated as Medieval currency. Up until the middle of the 18th century, it was part of Sintra's payment of taxes to the monarchy—so highly valued by royalty that it was worth more to them than cash.

Thanks to the use of the locally made *queijo fresco*, a *queijada* made anywhere else in the country (or the world) can never be replicated.

Later, and well into the late 1970s and early 1980s, many families in the area still made them as a way of earning extra income, and they would often be sold in neighboring Cascais and Lisbon. Sapa and Casa Periquita are two of the most famous producers of factory-produced *queijada* in Sintra these days.

***

Pillow pastries

Sintra's Casa Periquita is the birthplace of *travesseiros*, a rectangular shaped flaky pastry filled with a mix of eggs, sugar, and almonds. Created in the 1940s, *travesseiros* quickly became a local pastry celebrity. Rectangular in shape, they look like pillows... so that's what they're called! Insider tip: they're especially delicious served warm.

***

The most storied stay in Iberia

The oldest hotel in the Iberian Peninsula, Lawrence's Hotel, established in 1764, is located in Sintra, and is still functioning. Lord Byron stayed here back in the day. Currently, it's a boutique hotel of 16 unique rooms that is well worthy of a stay or at least a meal. A visit here is like stepping back in time—if the past had all modern conveniences.

***

Algarve's best kept secret for artists and adventurers

About 20 minutes north of Silves is a little town called São Bartolomeu de Messines, which is where you'll find Figs on the Funcho.

Named for the fig trees that grow along the banks of the River Funcho here, this boutique accommodation in old farmhouses was restored by U.K. expats Cheryl and Graham Smith. The buildings were converted into modern, stylish, and spacious villas.

Enjoy the infinity pool overlooking the river and decking areas designed for dining, entertaining, and most importantly—relaxing under the carob trees. Winding pathways to the water's edge were created in the garden for easy access for canoeing, stand-up paddleboarding, and fishing.

Plus they offer special-interest packages, such as painting workshops led by experienced and qualified art tutors. Walking excursions are led along the panoramic river Funcho, passing vineyards, orange, carob, olive, and cork oak trees, and aromatic lavender and rosemary plants. And bird-watchers are spoilt for choice here.

✳✳✳

⊚ **Vendas Novas**

Home of Portugal's most iconic sandwich

Not far from Setúbal lies the little town of Vendas Novas, which is generally acknowledged to be the origin of the famous *bifana* sandwich that you'll find throughout the country... although several other towns make the same claim...

Thin slices of pork are marinated in a mixture of white wine, paprika, garlic, bay leaf, and vinegar, and slowly cooked, and served in a *papo seco*, a crusty type of roll. *Bifana* is among the top three most widespread and beloved dishes in Portugal, after *bacalhau* (salted cod) and pastel de nata. They have even caught the attention of celebrity chefs Anthony Bourdain and Gordon Ramsay. Found in almost every corner of the country, often sold in small restaurants and cafés, this delectable pork sandwich is equally simple and complex.

Bifanas can be a quick meal or a snack, while also being an all-time favorite at the end of a night of drinking... You'll also see people having them for lunch with bowls of soup on the side.

As with anything prepared in different regions, there are variations to the *bifana*, but if you're looking to try the original—head to Vendas Novas.

✳✳✳

Southern Portugal

⦿ Cacela Velha

The secret to scoring a seaside table

The best way to get a table at the coveted seaside restaurants of Cacela Velha, where, in the summer, it seems sometimes that everyone and their mother is trying to eat?

There are two very popular restaurants with outdoor tables next to the village church that serve oysters and other seafood dishes...

You can't book a table at these over the phone. The trick is to arrive before you're hungry, get your name onto the restaurant's waiting list, and then enjoy a beer or two while savoring the views over the water. If you don't have the patience to wait for a table, you can order takeaway oysters.

***

⦿ Carvoeiro

Eat in a doll's house

"A Boneca" is a charming little beach bar and restaurant that's nestled in a little rocky inlet on the water a few minutes from Carvoeiro. Best reached by hiking the boardwalk on the cliffs, you'll also discover several naturally made rock formations along this little stretch of coast. The restaurant name means "the doll," which refers to the rock formations around the corner. Local fishermen thought it looked like a doll's house—indeed, you can go inside and look out its little windows to the sea. It's almost like a tree house, but made of hewn rock. Enjoy fresh seafood and refreshing cocktails, but expect to wait for a table if you go at mealtime, and don't expect the fastest service. The food is good, but this is a place to come and enjoy a leisurely rest in a stunning location more than it is about the eating.

***

⦿ **Faro**

Best pit stop on a hike in Ludo Park

In Ludo Park, just outside of Faro, there's an attractive lakeside restaurant called "The Shack," which opens around March or April and closes in November. It's a great rest stop for hikers in the park. In spring and autumn, it's best to call them to check whether they're open.

***

The best cheesecake in Faro

The Chelsea café in the pedestrian part of Praia da Luz. This busy establishment serves the best cheesecake in Faro.

***

Faro's finest cocktails with a view

"Columbus Bar," a Faro institution, is famous for its cocktails and sweeping view of the marina. And the venue itself is a worthy destination for those who appreciate architecture and history, tucked away as it is in the arcade of a 16th century hospital. Once just an evening destination, a few years ago this spot began serving during the day.

Meals are designed to be shared, and the fusion style is inspired by South American and Asian cuisine. In typical tapas style, there are no starters or mains, just lots of good dishes to be enjoyed in good company. Except for an Italian cheese, everything made here is locally sourced, seafood delivered daily from the river, oysters caught hours before ending up on your plate. And the chef has conceived everything to pair with the bar's famous cocktails.

Because it's the cocktails that this place is known for… a house specialty for almost 20 years, these concoctions have earned them several awards, including Best Bar Team and Best Cocktail Menu.

Plus, with music on Sunday nights and DJ sets after dinner from Wednesday to Sunday, this is a great place to spend just about any evening in Faro. The best way to enjoy an evening here is to arrive late afternoon to get a good table, enjoy a drink, indulge in a leisurely dinner, then dance the night away fueled by the best cocktails in town.

⦿ Ferragudo

Ferragudo's top spot for seafood and scenery

Rui's bar in Ferragudo, also known as The Yacht Club, on the main beach in town, is a lovely beach bar to sit and watch the world go by. Get the *cataplana* (fish soup).

⦿ Guia

Dining on the dunes

In Guia, next to Albufeira, "Restaurante Os Salgados" at Praia dos Salgados is a top choice in a wonderful location. It has a very relaxed atmosphere, with amazing fish and seafood, plus outstanding service. Not to mention a beachside bar area facing the dunes and the ocean.

***

From fishing hut to fine dining

Just down the coast, "Restaurante Lourenço" at Praia de Manuel Lourenço has fantastic quality food and personal service. Specializing in seafood and traditional Portuguese dishes, this is a perfect place to enjoy panoramic beach views as you eat.

***

⦿ Moncarapacho

Europe's only special needs holiday retreat

This is mainland Europe's only specialist holiday centre which is fully equipped to allow people with special needs young and old to experience a wonderful holiday with their family or carers.

***

⑨ **Monchique**

The best chicken you'll ever climb for

Aside from sardines, the best grilled food in southern Portugal has to be *frango no churrasco*, chicken from the grill. It comes two ways: *com* or *sem piri piri* (with or without piri piri). Try a bit of each. Chickens are farmed near the spa of Monchique, high up Mount Fóia from the coast, where it is traditional to hike, bike, or drive to special restaurants for your Sunday *frango*.

✳✳✳

Where the water heals

The Serra de Monchique is famous for its alkaline (it has a pH of about 9.5) and healthy spring water. Rich in fluoride, the water helps recover organic vitality. There are many fountains in the area from which the water gushes, and people fill up on natural mineral water in large bottles, especially in Caldas de Monchique.

✳✳✳

⑨ **Olhão**

The most inclusive menu in the Algarve

In the Algarve's Olhão, the restaurant "Chá Chá Chá" is not to be missed. Tucked away in an alley with indoor and outdoor tables, this authentic restaurant serves dishes with great depth of flavor, like marinated anchovies, tuna mayonnaise, and a cheese that arrives wrapped in an exotic leaf. Aside from having options for vegetarians, vegans, and celiacs, the food here is as fresh as can be, and deliciously prepared.

As the expat owner says, "Our great joy in living here and working here at "Chá Chá Chá" is to visit the market first thing in the morning, where we buy exceptionally fresh, locally caught fish at reasonable prices. My conversations with the fishermen start around midnight to discuss who is going out to sea. We won't look at fish that hasn't been caught that morning… So the lovely thing about being here is one becomes more attuned to, in tune with, the weather, the tides, the seasons, the local emotions."

***

The always-busy bakery

Olhão's bakery, café, and restaurant called Delícia de Olhão on the waterfront (Avenue 5 de Outubro), is a bustling place, even in winter, with customers drawn by its range of pastries.

⦿ **Porches**

Eat like a local, pay like a local

A go-to, day-to-day restaurant is a family-run place in Porches called "Ti Teresa." Everything is freshly cooked, the portions are generous, and they serve honest, home-cooked food, which is terrific value for money.

⦿ **Praia da Luz**

Luz's most elegant Sunday lunch

The Praia da Luz Fortaleza restaurant has a magnificent setting with exceptional cuisine. Open seven days a week for dinner, their four-course Sunday lunch with live jazz is a wonderful way to enjoy the setting.

***

Where tourists won't wander

For traditional Portuguese fare just outside of Praia da Luz, head to Burgau and the "Restaurante Ancora."

***

Best Indian food in Praia da Luz

Just outside Praia da Luz is "Spice Cottage," an excellent Indian restaurant.

***

Faro's most iconic sunset view

In Praia da Luz, one traditional destination in town is the rooftop terrace bar at the Hotel Faro, a favored spot to watch the sun set over the lagoon.

***

Algarve gin, rooted in tradition

Created by two locals and an expat, Alma Gin was born in Luz, made with five main ingredients to create the perfect spirit: juniper berries, coriander seeds, angelica root, cassia bark, and orris root, and produced in a traditional Portuguese-made copper still.

***

⦿ Praia da Rocha

The best tapas spot in Praia da Rocha

Head to "Sanleti," right off the beach. Prepared with a passion for local dishes and wine accompaniments, these Portuguese twists on tapas aren't just snacks, they are meal worthy. Everything is fresh and homemade, but also innovative and creative.

⦿ Silves

Silves' most time-honored coffee spot

Café "Da Rosa," just beside the Medieval Arch in a pretty square, is the best café in Silves. It's one of the most authentic and traditional Portuguese cafés in town. It has been serving quality coffees for over 40 years, and the setting is perfect. Check out the tiled walls inside, too.

***

Music, meals, and medieval walls

If music is your thing, situated just below the Silves castle walls is "Café Inglês," famous for its live music on Sunday afternoons. Enjoy a leisurely meal while listening to jazz. The restaurant hosts jazz, Latin, African, and other types of live music during the week.

***

Best piri piri chicken in the south

In Silves at mealtime, most people gravitate to the waterfront and head to "Churrasqueira Valdemar" beside the market. The rumor is that they do the best piri-piri chicken in the whole of the Algarve.

***

The most worthwhile wrong turn in Silves

For fish connoisseurs, try "Marisqueira Rui" in Silves, tucked in one of the side streets for traditional and reasonably priced meals.

***

Finest farm-to-farmhouse meal

Just outside of Silves is "Restaurante O Barradas," the perfect place to enjoy authentic Portuguese fare. It's located in a converted farmhouse, just a few kilometers away from Silves. They serve dishes like slow-cooked suckling pig and octopus served on a bed of sweet potato mash.

***

Hidden dining under historic castle walls

Head to the "Recanto dos Mouros" restaurant hidden away behind Silves Castle. The views over the citrus orchards make this a special location for a meal.

***

A taste of France in the Algarve

Wine lovers will enjoy Quinta do Francês Winery. This is a 19-acre (7.69-hectare) family-owned vineyard estate that can be found right at the base of the hills of Silves. You can enjoy beautiful views of the surrounding countryside from their exclusive location.

They have a wine shop and tasting room on-site where you can buy their products as well as regional products. They offer guided tours of their winery and cellar where you can learn more about the owner, Patrick Agostini, a French doctor, who had a dream about creating his own vineyard. He produces the award-winning Quinta do Francês Odelouca River Valley and Odelouca (red, white, and rosé) on-site.

***

The prettiest sweets in Silves

Morgadinhos, little round-shaped treats made with ground almonds, sugar, and egg yolks, are said to come from the Silves and Portimão area. In these, pearly-white layer of marzipan hides one layer of chila/gila (pumpkin) jam, one layer of egg cream, and one layer of egg strands. A must-try if you have a big sweet tooth!

***

⊚ **São Brás**

The best meals are outside the map

Near São Brás, inland of the Algarve coast, some of the best local restaurants are scattered outside the town itself. Check out the stylish "Lagar da Mesquita" eatery and "Rocha da Gralheira," perched high with views of the hills.

***

⊚ **Tavira**

Octopus any way you want it

Near Tavira, Santa Luzia's "Casa do Polvo" (House of Octopus) offers octopus anyway you can think of. Spicy octopus samosa, fried octopus croquette, pasty filled with octopus, octopus carpaccio, octopus salad with tomato, octopus roe salad, octopus rice, octopus curry, octopus stew with beans… and pretty much any other octopus dish you could imagine…

***

Where monks once walked—now, you dine

Get lunch in the courtyard of the historic Pousada Convento de Tavira, an upmarket hotel that has been the site of both a synagogue and a Christian religious house. At lunch in the tranquil courtyard, you can savor *muxama*, dry-cured tuna loin, a southern Iberia specialty.

If you're looking for a nice place to stay here, this hotel is a top choice.

***

⦿ Vilamoura

The best door-to-steak transfer in town

"Bovino Steakhouse" in Quinta do Lago near Vilamoura will never disappoint. The location, the service, the food, the golf cart that collects you from the car park and escorts you to the entrance. It's superb.

***

⦿ Vila Real de Santo António

Best Italian food in Vila Real de Santo António

The best restaurant in Vila Real de Santo António is "Ernesto," according to the many Italian expats of the town. You may have guessed it—the owner is Italian, from near Rome, to be precise, and the menu is proudly Italian. Dishes include the Neapolitan classic spaghetti with clams, carpaccio of Uruguayan beef, and oysters with gin and lime. Ernesto is on the waterfront avenue, and you can eat outside, under an awning, and contemplate the views of the river and the boats bobbing in the water.

The Islands

⌖ Azores

The star of the show

On Graciosa, one of the islands in the Azores archipelago, another version of Sintra's famous *queijada* (cheesecake) is made, this one in a star shape.

*****

⌖ Madeira

Laurel-branch kebabs

In Madeira, try *espetada*, which is chunks of beef skewered (traditionally with laurel branches) and fire-roasted.

*****

More than just bread

A Madeiran speciality is *bolo do caco*, a local garlic bread served with most meals. The bread is flat and circular, with a chewy, soft texture and an almost sweet taste. Locals say that this is because the fresh Madeira water that's mixed into the dough is so pure…

*****

Packing a punch

You can thank Infante D. Henrique for Madeira's traditional libation, *poncha*. On his order in 1425, sugar cane (from Sicily) was introduced to the newly colonized island. From cane syrup came Madeiran rum, called *rhum agricole*, not to be confused with the molasses-based *rhum industriel*. *Rhum agricole* is matured in Madeira-fortified wine casks, giving it a depth of flavor. The origins of *poncha*, however, are unclear.

Poncha is just like punch (in fact, that's where we get the name for punch), but with a serious kick. It consists of cane-sugar alcohol mixed with honey and fruit juice—lemon, orange, passion fruit… even banana. Locals claim *poncha* can cure colds.

Just outside of Funchal proper, Camara do Lobos is ground zero for the gold standard *poncha à pescador* (fisherman's *poncha*). But its origins, or at least inspiration, may have been an Indian drink called *pãnch/panch*. It's also thought that *poncha* is the forerunner of the well-loved Brazilian cocktail, caipirinha.

Best served with peanuts or lupines, this strong, fruity punch can easily be replicated at home.

***

The ultimate wine tour

When in Madeira, you've got to try Madeira wine. You can try the fortified wine produced only here at tastings across the island. The most famous is Blandy's Wine Lodge, where you'll get intimate knowledge of the Madeira-making process.

National Bests

Some of Portugal's best dishes aren't necessarily traceable back to their region of origin… but we'd be remiss not to include them…

Order in like a local

No matter how much we love to eat out, sometimes we all just want to order in and eat on the couch. When you're too exhausted from exploring all day, use Glovo, a food-delivery app similar to Seamless or Grubhub.

***

Salted legacy: Portugal's cod chronicles

Bacalhau (cod): The national dish of Portugal and the ultimate local delicacy—perhaps even obsession! Cod is an extremely versatile fish, and in Portugal, they say they have 1,001 recipes for it (at the very least 365—one for each day of the year).

For centuries, the Portuguese have dried cod and covered it in salt as a way of preserving it for long periods (and before fridges were invented). Today, you can buy cod already desalted and hydrated, but locals like to be in charge of this process.

Bacalhau refers to the dried and salted cod. The drying process takes several days and gives you a tasty, tender fish that can be cooked in many ways, including grilled, baked in the oven, or fried in the pan.

Even though it's not fished off the coast of Portugal, *bacalhau* is considered one of Portugal's national treasures. It's sold in stores everywhere and has a pungent scent.

You'll find a large variety that differs in color, size, smell, taste, and dryness. Such variation has led Portugal to define requirements as to what products can carry the label "*Bacalhau de Cura Tradicional Portuguesa.*"

They are graded by weight, which often defines what price category the *bacalhau* is sold under:

* Especial (more than 4 kgs)
* Graúdo (4 to 2 kgs)
* Crescido (2 to 1 kgs)
* Corrente (1 to 0.5 kgs)
* Miúdo (below 500 grams)

Eaten all kinds of ways and at all times of year, cod is the quintessential item on Portuguese tables on Christmas Eve.

How to desalt your own cod like a local:

Simply put the cod in a container with water (enough to cover the fish) and place it in the fridge. Make sure to discard that water and renew it about twice a day for 24 to 48 hours, depending on your preference and the thickness of the cut.

How to eat it the traditional way:

Families eat cod prepared as simply as possible: boiled with a side of vegetables like potatoes, carrots, turnips, and cabbage. You might add a sprinkle of finely chopped raw garlic... and you should definitely add a generous drizzle of olive oil.

How to eat it the indulgent way:

Bacalhau com natas (literally "cod with cream") is baked in the oven and comes out as layers of flaky *bacalhau*, onion, fried potato, and cream, topped with cheese, and served piping hot. It's creamy, rich, and decadent tasting.

How to eat it the seasonal (and simplest) way:

Bacalhau à lagareiro has become a popular choice as a simple and delicious way to eat cod, showcasing the fish and the sparing ingredients used to bring out its flavor. Easy to prepare, this recipe used to be associated with the olive harvest and the pressing of new olive oil, especially in Central Portugal. The olive presses are called *lagar* in Portuguese, and *lagareiro* is—you guessed it—the owner of the presses. Needless to say, this recipe calls for lots and lots of olive oil… and little else.

✳✳✳

Grilled glory: the fish that rules the summer

You can't get away from sardines in Portugal—if it's summer, they're on every grill and menu, and even when they aren't in season, you'll find them tinned and sold everywhere. The Portuguese eat an amazing 12 pounds of sardines per person per year.

Grilled sardines or *sardinhas asadas* are a local staple, traditionally eaten wedged between two slices of white bread and eaten whole—head and all.

The best time to eat fresh sardines is between June and August—best served straight from the charcoal grill, marinated with Portuguese olive oil, alongside salad, rice, and potatoes.

In restaurants, they are ultra-fresh, simply given a dash of salt (big or Kosher salt, not table salt), and tossed on the barbie. They are served with small red boiled potatoes and eaten with a fish fork and knife.

You slit the critter down its backbone, remove the skin, extract the fillet from the bone, head, and tail, and eat it. Then the other fillet. Turn it over and repeat. By the 24th fillet, you will have mastered the knack.

Fresh sardines are good for you as their oil is full of good cholesterol. Nothing out of a can comes close to tasting as good.

***

Spice route to the soul of Portuguese flavor

When Portuguese settlers in Africa came upon the small, hot, African bird's eye chili, they did what any food lover would do: combined it with garlic, oil, and vinegar to make a taste sensation, piri-piri sauce.

Fantastic on grilled chicken, it's equally delicious on roasted cashews, dribbled on popcorn, or as a marinade for shrimp. Recipes vary by region and cook. You'll find piri-piri oil, piri-piri paste, or piri-piri-sauce.

***

Born of fire: Portugal's pride on a plate

Chicken piri piri is created when the piri-piri or peri-peri pepper is used to coat the skins of chicken legs and wings, served with a portion of fries and a side salad. The chicken is spatchcocked and marinaded in a sauce made of garlic, olive oil, salt, lemon juice, and piri-piri. Restaurants then grill the chicken over a coal barbecue, which adds to the flavor. Grab the chicken with your hands and gnaw away at it… don't stand on ceremony with this one.

***

The crunchy king of Portuguese snacks

Bacalhau fritters, *pataniscas*, or *pastel de bacalhau*, are ubiquitous in snack bars across Portugal. Perfect for *lanche*, that Portuguese pseudo-meal typically eaten between lunch and dinner, these fritters are stuffed with shredded salt cod and fried to crunch perfection. New versions can come with cheese, but these aren't the traditional recipe. Great with an ice-cold Sagres or Super Bock beer, you might have to make the rounds in search of your favorite *patanisca* or create your own little *lanche* spread at home.

***

Portugal's answer to prosciutto

Presunto is the Portuguese cousin of the more famous Spanish *jamón* and the Italian *prosciutto*, with deep roots in Portuguese culinary tradition and often associated with celebrations.

Its production in what is now Portugal goes back to, at least, the time of the Romans, and its long shelf life made it a staple in ships during the Discoveries. There are different varieties of *presunto* in Portugal, with some regions being particularly renowned for theirs, such as Alentejo and Beira Interior. Quality is informed by the breed of the pig, its diet, and the meat's curing process.

In most cases, *presunto* is smoked, but in areas with low humidity, like in the Alentejo, it's left to dry instead. The process can take more than a year, depending on the desired flavor and texture.

Most Portuguese prefer to eat *presunto* simple, or often with a generous slice of bread or cheese. Extra points if both the bread and the cheese are from the same region as the *presunto*.

You can also add it to any charcuterie board or prepare a quick, refreshing summer appetizer with slices of melon wrapped up in thin slices of *presunto*.

Or enjoy your *presunto* cooked. It can be either grilled or fried or used as part of more or less complex dishes. You'll usually find it as a topping for soups, for example, or mixed with other ingredients, like minced meat in savory pies.

***

Fish bait to beer mate

Tremoços, or lupin beans, are only used as fish bait in most countries. In Portugal, they are brined and put out as a snack to accompany a beer. While it's true they don't have a lot of flavor, the humble lupin bean is packed full of nutritional benefits. Removing the peel using your teeth is a fine art that any Portuguese will gladly teach you. As well as being given a small dish with a drink, you might see these on *petiscos* (tapas) menus.

***

Slow food at its finest

Caracóis, snails, are appreciated in Portugal as they are in France: as a yummy snack. In Portugal, spring and summer are "snail season." Look for cafés and snack bars displaying a *"temos caracóis"* (we have snails) sign or a simple snail drawing to advertise them. When in season, they're often sold as *petiscos* (tapas).

***

The snack that will keep you pecking

Pica pau, literally, "woodpecker," is made with chunks of beef marinated in white wine and garlic and then fried and served with pickles and plenty of sauce (for dipping your bread). Why the name? Because *pica pau* is meant to be "pecked" with a toothpick. You'll come across it when you're out for *petiscos* (tapas).

***

Portugal's most deceptive dish

Beware of ordering vegetables by accident… The Portuguese are so enamored of seafood, they've named other foods after it.

Peixinhos da horta translates to "little fish from the vegetable garden." But this dish has nothing to do with seafood. These are green beans dipped in a light batter and deep-fried until crispy. Sometimes you'll also find them served as a light meal, with a side of tomato rice. A common *petiscos* (tapas) dish.

***

Tapas and a show

Chouriço assado, or flame-grilled sausage, is a fun way to enjoy your snack. The waiter brings the *chouriço* to the table in a special clay dish that serves as a container for a mix of alcohol brandy and which has a type of clay "bars" where the *chouriço* is placed. The waiter then sets the alcohol on fire, and in a matter of minutes, you get crispy grilled *chouriço*, right in front of you. Often seen on *petiscos* (tapas) menus.

***

Gizzards with gusto

Moelas are chicken gizzards slowly cooked in a tomato sauce with onions, garlic, and spices. It's a common *petisco* (tapa) dish. Don't knock it until you've tried it!

✳✳✳

Sea monsters on a plate

Percebes, goose barnacles, are boiled and usually sold by weight as a *petisco* (tapa) dish. They have to be the strangest looking boil up you'll have seen.

✳✳✳

Non-calamari

While you might see squid or octopus on local menus, you'll probably also come across *choco frito*. Not to be confused with some kind of chocolate, these are strips of cuttlefish that are seasoned, breaded, and deep-fried until golden and crispy, often served with a wedge of lemon, just like calamari.

✳✳✳

Ancient Rome's sweet legacy

Filhós de laranja, fried dough made with flour, sugar, orange, and vanilla, go hand in hand with *carnival*.

Also known more generally as *filhoses*, they may look like donuts, fritters, or donut holes, and they are inseparable from this time of year. Whether you call it Shrove Tuesday, Pancake Day, *carnival*, etc., fried dough is what you eat in Europe.

The tradition goes back to the Romans, who would eat *frictilia*, a type of fritter made from spelt flour, eggs, ground pepper, honey, and poppy seeds during Saturnalia.

Portuguese *filhoses* are the modern version of this ancient treat. The main difference is the fact that we add a generous sprinkle of powdered cinnamon. In some places, they like to add a shot of *aguardente* to the batter… and instead of lemon zest, for example, you could add orange zest.

✳✳✳

Divine desserts from Portugal's convents

Doces conventuais, or "conventual sweets" were created by nuns in the 15th century and earlier. They are famous for their richness and egg yolk is usually the most prevalent ingredient.

Back when convents and monasteries had to be as self-sufficient as possible, they raised chickens, which led to an abundance of eggs. Egg whites had many uses, including clearing wine and stiffening clothes… which left a surplus of yolks.

Clever bakers put them to use in baking and confectionaries. Many of the country's most famous sweets have names reflecting their religious origin: *toucinho do céu* (heaven's bacon), *papos de anjo* (angel's chins), and *barrigas de freira* (nun's bellies), to name a few.

Sugar and spices were fairly easy to access via Africa and Asia but still expensive, which made these desserts special and distinctive—perfect to be sold or offered to wealthy visitors and patrons of those convents and monasteries.

In 1820, however, the Liberal Revolution ousted religious orders from Portugal, and the recipes for these sweets left the secrecy of religious institutions.

Some of the recipes were sold, but some were already known, as wealthy families usually sent their daughters to convents for their education. They simply became slightly more democratic.

Several of these sweets also made their way to other parts of the globe, where they were adapted, like the Portuguese *fios de ovos*, which became Thailand's *foi thong*.

Another example is the Portuguese *brisas do Lis*, which became *quindim* in Brazil. The main difference? The Portuguese use almond meal, and Brazilians use shredded coconut.

*****

Portugal's most hearty hug in a bowl

Portuguese comfort food? Cozy and satisfying, like a hearty American chili, *feijoada* (*feijão* means beans) is a bean and meat stew that will stick to your ribs, traditionally made with homemade products and what the land produces. While Portugal introduced *feijoada* to Brazil, where black beans are featured, you will usually see Portuguese *feijoadas* with white (often Azorean) or red beans.

***

The sweetest way to say thanks

Queijinhos, literally, "little cheeses," have nothing to do with cheese. They'll either be *queijinhos de amêndoa* (little almond cheeses) or *queijinhos de figo* (little fig cheeses). The former are made with an almond paste and filled with egg cream; the latter are made with dried figs, sugar, almonds, cocoa powder, and spices. Quite often, they also include carob powder.

Both *queijinhos* are shaped like—you guessed it—little round cheeses. These are traditionally eaten on May 1 or made as gifts for especially helpful neighbors or doctors, for example.

***

The taste of grandma's kitchen

Arroz doce, sweet rice, aka rice pudding, is loved across Portugal and found in homes and eating establishments across the country. It makes sense, considering Portugal's rice culture, where the per capita rice consumption is a whopping 16+ kilograms per person annually. The short-grained, velvety-when-cooked, Portuguese-grown Carolino variety absorbs the flavors it's cooked in, making it a perfect partner for *arroz doce*. A whiff or taste of this simple, warm, cinnamon-y dessert is sure to send you back to childhood in your grandmother's kitchen.

***

The summeriest side dish

Pimentos assados (roasted peppers) are a common side dish during summer. Often found in Portuguese restaurants and homes, they're usually served alongside grilled fish, like sardines and mackerel. Summer is when peppers are in season, so preparing them in the warmer months of the year helps guarantee the best possible taste. Although *pimentos assados* are more popular in the southern regions of Portugal, their popularity has spread throughout the country.

***

The most autumnal snack in Portugal

In most towns and cities, as soon as summer ends, ice cream carts give way to roasted chestnut carts. Known as *castanhas* in Portuguese, chestnuts have a significant place in Portugal's autumn traditions as well as a long historical background. Whether roasted, as part of hearty dishes, or used in desserts and baking, chestnuts have a pivotal role in much of the Portuguese gastronomy.

***

The meatiest looking dessert

Salame de chocolate, a favorite at children's parties but also seen at Christmas festivities, is a mix of chocolate, butter, biscuits, and sometimes nuts, which is then shaped like a roll and served cold and cut into slices. It looks exactly like a link of salami and slices of sausage on a plate!

***

Fried, filled, and festa-ready

At any *festa* across the country, you'll find *churros* and *farturas*… They are similar, but distinct—here's how to tell the difference.

Churros are rolled in sugar and cinnamon, and you can either get the small ones (in paper bags with 6 or 12 *churros*) or you can have a bigger one with a filling of your choice (strawberry, sweet condensed milk, chocolate, mint, and egg cream are among the most popular options).

Farturas are a bit softer than churros, are spiral-shaped, cut into large pieces, and dusted with sugar and cinnamon. Both are best enjoyed still warm.

***

Portugal's take on sangria

Even if you've never set foot in Portugal (or Spain) there's a good chance you've drunk sangria... The word sangria literally means blood-letting and is a clear reference to red wine, used in the traditional version of this drink.

Although the meaning of the name is obvious, the origins of this Iberian drink are not completely clear: some claim it originated during the Roman period, while others believe it dates back to the times of the maritime discoveries.

Sangria shares a few things with many traditional drinks and dishes... recipes are usually mere guidelines; it has evolved and adapted to the times; there are many variants, from the simplest to quite elaborate ones. The Portuguese versions of sangria tend to rely heavily on lemons and oranges, which is a perfect excuse (in case you need one) to become acquainted with oranges from the Algarve, famous for their juicy sweetness.

*****

Camino comforts: budget beds and holy stamps

Hostels for pilgrims on the Camino de Santiago are called *albergues*. These are usually basic hostels with dormitories and shared facilities. To prove you're a pilgrim you need to show your Credential and you get a stamp at every *albergue* you stay in. There are two types: the municipal ones are cheaper, usually priced between 5 to 6 euros per person per night, but they can't be booked in advance. Private *albergues* are more expensive, between 10 to 12 euros per person per night. These usually have better facilities and can be booked in advance over the phone or via online booking service.

2. Shopping

Whether it's the best spot for organic produce, the place to find books in English, or the best place to find a 15th century manuscript, Portugal has some fantastic shopping options... let us introduce you to a few of our most notable favorites.

Northern Portugal

⌖ Porto

The storefront that time forgot (but locals never did)

In Porto, "A Pérola do Bolhão," which has been open since 1917, is a fantastic place to buy local and gourmet products. From mountain cheeses and sausages to wines and fruits, this is a great place to bring visitors or to find local products to take back for loved ones. And its façade is probably the most photographed in the city…

***

Porto's market of many delights

Mercado Do Bom Sucesso in Porto is a fun new-concept multi-use space, offering dozens of stalls full of gastronomic delights from all over Portugal and beyond. These food stalls make up a modern, upscale "food court," interspersed with shops selling clothes, books, fresh-food stalls, local specialties, and more.

Weekly events are held here, from intimate live concerts, DJ sets, and theater and dance performances to exhibitions and educational workshops for both children and adults.

***

From tiles to tomatoes: Porto's most authentic market

Dating back to 1850, Mercado Do Bolhão is known for the monumentality of its neoclassic architecture and for having the freshest products in town—many nearby restaurants get their ingredients exclusively from this market. Despite recent renovations, the classic look of the building has been retained and as many of the original tiles have been preserved as possible. The building and the experience of shopping here is the essence of Porto and one of the best places to experience the true Porto lifestyle. It's not just Porto's most iconic market, it's also one of the most famous in the entire country.

***

Grocery GPS: Finding Your Essentials In Portugal

When it comes to settling into the day to day of Portugal, whether as a visitor or a tourist, you'll need to pick up the essentials—here's how to parse the supermarkets you'll find here...

- ❖ For gourmet and high-end grocery products along with everyday items, make sure to check out Supercor.
- ❖ Of the three main grocery stores you'll find across the country, Pingo Doce, Minipreço, and Continente Bom Dia, Miniprecio has the lowest prices.
- ❖ Inter-Marché is a French supermarket with wide selection of goods.
- ❖ Low-cost chains like Lidl and Aldi are great for stocking up on cheaper items.
- ❖ Apolónia is a more exclusive (and expensive) option for shopping.
- ❖ For British items, check the Overseas Supermarkets (several location in Algarve), which exclusively sell English products.

***

A temple of tales: Inside Portugal's most beautiful bookstore

Porto's Livraria Lello is considered one of the most beautiful book-

stores in the world and certainly the most emblematic in Portugal. It has been a huge inspiration for writers and artists from all over the world, including "Harry Potter" author J. K. Rowling, who was a regular guest while she lived in Porto. It was the famous wooden staircases of Lello that inspired her vision of the Hogwarts' stairs, and Porto University's student uniforms (which aren't very different from those worn by all Portuguese students) that inspired the long black coats of the Hogwarts's uniforms.

****

From queens to keepsakes: The north's finest filigree

Although nowadays you get filigree virtually anywhere in Portugal, it really comes from the north of Portugal and is an important part of the traditional wedding dresses from the northernmost Minho region. Filigree is the art of working delicate gold and silver threads, finely intertwined to form elaborate pieces. Entirely handmade, it requires an immense degree of patience and skill from goldsmiths. The most famous filigree design is the "Heart of Viana" pendant, which has its origins in a commission made by Queen Dona Maria I (1734-1816). If you're not in the market for a wedding dress, you can get filigree as earrings or brooches, too.

****

Most tangled treasure in the north

In Portugal, *bilros* lace is connected to the fishing areas of the coast, with written references from 1616 to *bilros* lace makers. *Bilros* is very delicate, with a variety of stitches and patterns that allow for a huge diversity of results.

To the women in fishing villages, *bilros* became a viable subsistence activity, especially when the men were away fishing or emigrated. Little towns like Póvoa de Varzim and Vila do Conde in the north, Peniche and Sesimbra on the central coast around Lisbon, and Lagos in the south have a strong tradition in this type of embroidery. You might find it in other places, including inland, but the tradition is strongest near the sea. Vila do Conde claims a special relationship with the art and even has an annual craft fair and museum dedicated to it, where you can watch artists weave and learn how to do it yourself. Watching an artisan making *bilros* lace is nothing short of mind-blowing!

Central Portugal

⦿ Caldas da Rainha

Caldas's tastiest time machine

Looking for a gourmet shop in Caldas da Rainha where you can buy some local goodies, like biscuits, jams, cheese, or fruit liqueurs? Head over to "Mercearia Pena," a specialty shop that's been open since 1909. It's the perfect spot to get gifts for when you go for a visit back home.

***

The only daily farmer's market in Portugal

The Praça da Fruta (Fruit Market) in Caldas da Rainha is located in Praça da República, in the town center, and is the country's only daily outdoor farmer's market. This historic market has been operating in the same place since the 15th century and still opens from 8 a.m. to 1 p.m. every day. Here you'll find fresh produce, flowers, cheese, sweets, smoked and cured meats, as well as dried fruits and nuts.

***

⦿ Cascais

The greenest grocers on the coast

Miosótis, Mundo Bio, Bioshop Cascais, and Go Natural are all located in the Cascais/Estoril area and stock organic produce, groceries, and many household and beauty products.

***

The mightiest market in Cascais

The enormous Cascais market, Mercado de Vila, on Wednesdays and Saturdays, with fishmongers, bakers, butcher shops, and the freshest seasonal produce you can find at prices easy on the wallet, is a favorite for locals and expats. There's also a flea market on Wednesdays and a craft market on Saturdays with an organic stall. It also hosts events above and beyond markets.

***

English book nook by the sea

If it's English-language books you're looking for, Cascais has a great option: look no further than the used bookshop in the Cascais Citadel, Deja Lu. It has one of the largest selections around.

***

⦿ Lisbon

The best of the east in the heart of Lisbon

For spices and Asian grocery products in general (including some fresh produce) browse through the little shops in the Martim Moniz and Mouraria neighborhoods of Lisbon.

***

From farm to fair trade: Almada's eco market

On the last weekend of every month, from March to November, Parque da Paz in Alamda (just across the Ponte 25 de Abril from Lisbon), hosts the Almada Green Market. Dedicated to promoting sustainable consumption, this market gathers dozens of local agricultural produc-ers, artisans, and artists to showcase local products.

Shop for freshly picked produce, plants, natural cosmetics, honey and vegan ice cream, and much more. Find Fair Trade certified products and a wide range of ecological, zero-waste items, and goods made of recycled materials. This market has also become a venue for workshops and free activities as well as art exhibits.

***

The Real Aisles Of Portugal

While there is no shortage of modern grocery stores in Portugal, you'll find that markets are the heart of the local food shopping scene, and you'll find several markets in each district.

The market is one of the Portuguese people's favorite ways to buy fresh produce, sometimes straight from the farmer. They offer not just fruit, fresh fish, and vegetables but also local products like cheese, smoked sausages, and bread. Many of them also have butcher shops and florists. (And frequenting them is one of the best ways to feel integrated in the local community.)

Where the locals still shop—Lisbon's least famous markets

The most visited Lisbon market is Mercado da Ribeira, the "Time Out Market," which is not only sponsored but looks more like a temple than a market and is located right on the water—hence its fame and popularity.

But other neighborhoods also have wonderful markets, too. They all offer local produce, as well as fresh fish and seafood, meat, flowers, dried fruits, nuts, and spices, but some are famous for certain items, for example Saldanha market for spices, or Alvalade, known for its produce selection. Head to Campo de Ourique for a market-meets-food-court experience, Princípe Real for organics every Saturday or flea market on the last weekend of the month, Benfica for fantastic handicrafts, or Arroios for a community-driven market.

*****

The world's oldest bookstore, still in print since 1732

Livraria Bertrand in Lisbon's Chiado neighborhood was founded in 1732, making it the oldest bookstore in the world. Today, the chain has another 58 branches across the country. This cavernous store has room after room of books, including an English section, kids' sections, and a section of translated books featuring Portugal and by Portuguese authors. In the far back, you'll find a café with some indoor and outdoor seating. If you buy a book here, you'll be offered the store's famous stamp in either English or Portuguese, which is a must-do.

***

The bookstore with the most secrets

Livraria Sa da Costa, just a couple blocks from Livraria Bertrand, opened its doors in 1913… so it's not nearly as old as its famous neighbor… but it has more than enough character to make up for it. Part bookshop, part antique store, part curio selection, part museum-worthy collection of books, this place is a treasure trove that you could spend hours rifling through.

Aside from being a shop with newly published books, the store owns texts from the beginning of printing in the 15th century, manuscripts, rare books from the 15th to the 20th century, and out-of-print books from the 20th and 21st centuries. They even allow students, researchers, and book lovers in general to access historical texts in all areas of human knowledge, which would otherwise be unavailable for purchase and only partially available for consultation in public libraries.

The store also promotes events in the gallery above the store, such as painting, sculpture and jewelry exhibitions, workshops, and book launches.

***

The bookshop that always says yes

Just a couple blocks from the sea, Salted Books in Lisbon is not just an English bookstore, it supplies libraries and schools in Portugal. There's plenty of inventory to browse in the store, but they also claim to be able to source any English book for you by request if you can't find it yourself.

***

⊚ Óbidos

The holiest bookshop in Portugal (literally)

Igreja De São Tiago (Church Of São Tiago) in Óbidos was originally built in 1186, eventually donated to the municipality in 1989 and is now... a bookshop. Even if you're not interested in buying any books, it's worth stepping in to see how well an old religious building was transformed into a modern bookshop with unique displays.

***

From Moorish hands to modern homes: Portugal's most walkable masterpieces

Arraiolos, a little town about an hour and a half inland of Lisbon, makes rugs. Hand-embroidered with wool on jute or cotton fabric, these traditional items are works of art that have been made the same way for hundreds of years. The first reference to them dates back to 1598, and it is believed that their origin is linked to the Moors of Lisbon, expelled by D. Manuel I in 1496. On their way to Spain and North Africa, some of them settled in Arraiolos and kept working in their trades.

Although the method remains the same, the rug's decorative style has changed over time. You can still find rugs with traditional motifs, such as flowers, animals, and vases, but new patterns have adopted geometric patterns and a minimalist style.

***

Portugal's Handmade Heritage—Not Your Average Tourist Trinkets

In a fast-paced world of instant everything, Portugal's handcrafted treasures are slow, soulful, and steeped in story.

From golden filigree to hand-stitched rugs, these time-honored arts carry echoes of centuries past—crafted with techniques passed down through generations and shaped by the landscapes, legends, and lives of their regions.

Each piece is a labor of love—imperfect in all the right ways—and a beautiful reminder that sometimes, tradition really does do it best.

***

The nation's most noble needlework

Although its origins are uncertain, we know that Castelo Branco embroidery dates back to the 17th century, and it is believed to have been brought to the Portuguese court by Eastern embroiderers. Castelo Branco embroidery is made with colorful silk thread on linen canvas and uses a variety of fauna and flora designs, most of which have a symbolic meaning. Common traditional decorative elements include carnations, roses, lilies, grapes, vases, birds, and the biblical Tree of Life, among others. Traditionally, it's used to make incredibly elaborate quilts, but you can also find it in sachets and other smaller items.

***

⊚ Setúbal

Portugal's most picture-perfect market

Setúbal is famous for the Mercado do Livramento, a market that was considered by *USA Today* in 2015 as one of the most famous fish markets in the world. This municipal market offers not only fish and seafood but also fresh produce and meat, as well as Portuguese-style biscuits, honey, and preserves. More than that, it's a pleasure to visit because of its panels of hand-painted tiles (*azulejos*).

***

A feast for all the senses

Mercado da Conceição is a fun local market here, because it mixes traditional items with modern ones so well. It also includes a leisure area with food stalls, which makes it a great place to stop for a bite to eat. With a cultural and musical event calendar, this market has become as much a social meeting place and venue as much as a traditional market. It's open Tuesday to Sunday, from 7 a.m. to 3 p.m. and 5 p.m. to 11 p.m.

***

Where Setúbal gets its greens

The Mercado Biológico de Setúbal (Setúbal's Organic Market), takes place every Thursday, and shouldn't be missed for those who value fresh, organic produce.

***

⊚ **Sintra**

Farm-fresh at your front door

In Sintra, you can have fresh organic produce delivered to your doorstep. Check, for example, Quinta do Arneiro, Biocabaz, or Cooperativa Aldea.

***

Sintra's oldest open-air tradition

There's no shortage of markets in the Sintra municipality, but the most famous one is, without a doubt, the São Pedro de Sintra open-air market (open every second and fourth Sunday), which dates back to the 12th century. Here, you can find a bit of everything: fruit and vegetables, local bread and cakes, cured meats, olives, cheese, clothes, shoes, and plants. Don't miss the ladies baking *pão com chouriço* on the spot.

***

Southern Portugal

⊚ **Algoz**

Artisan market for wicker, wood, and whimsy

The flea market in Algoz is held in a large area near to the village hall. It occurs once a month on the second Monday of the month between 8 a.m. and 1 p.m. The market specializes in handmade goods such as wicker, wood, and ceramic items.

***

⦿ Aljezur

The best market for produce with provenance

Every Saturday from 7 a.m. to 1 p.m. in the main exhibition hall on the edge of the town, the Aljezur Farmers' Market sets up shop. Inside this cavernous venue you'll find produce so local it comes from the neighboring fields and farms. The vendors proudly tell you exactly how it was grown. Local fruit and vegetables, jams, bread and cakes, and local crafts are all on sale.

***

⦿ Boliqueime

The most welcoming community market

Boliqueime antiques fair is held monthly on the first Sunday of the month in an area near the churchyard in the village. Everyone is welcome to set up a stall. Sellers can bring pop-up tables or lay blankets on the floor to display their items. Contact the organizer, Alice (pop into her curiosity shop on Rua Prof. Jose Jorge Rodrigues, Boliqueime) to book a stall, arrange your license, and arrange payment. Buyers arrive about 8 a.m. and leave about 1 p.m.

***

⦿ Faro

Shop local in Faro

Faro Municipal Market is located in the center of the city and has a huge range of fish and meat for sale, alongside fruit and vegetables, olives, and other local products. Open Monday to Friday from 8:30 a.m. to 7 p.m. and Saturdays from 9 a.m. to 1 p.m.

***

⦿ Ferragudo

The Algarve's most browseable bazaar

For the monthly Ferragudo Flea Market, the streets of Ferragudo are filled with all manner of second-hand goods, garden tools, toys, jewelry, and antiques (the second Sunday of each month from 8 a.m. to 1 p.m.). Head for the main square and peruse the items, most of which are laid out on blankets and rugs on the ground. You can book a slot through the Junta de Freguesia.

***

⚲ Lagos

Where the farm comes to you

Every Saturday from 8 a.m. to 2 p.m., local farmers bring live chickens, olives, fruit and vegetables, homemade preserves and jams, and fresh flowers to town.

***

Straight from net to counter

For a great selection of local fresh fish, visit the municipal market opposite the marina. It's open Monday to Saturday, from 7 a.m. to 2 p.m.

***

The market with the most buzz (and craft beer)

On Wednesday evenings from 5 p.m. to 9 p.m. the organic Viv'o Mercado sets up opposite the main council buildings. The market focuses on organic food and goods, fresh veg, local craft beers and natural cosmetics, Algarve honey and jams, natural and zero-waste soaps and creams, traditional cakes and sweets, nuts, olives, and other local produce. It's not exclusively organic, so look out for sellers with the blue umbrellas to ensure you're getting local, organic produce. There are often food trucks and live music, too.

***

⚲ Loulé

One-stop-shop in an elegant market hall

Loulé market is located in the historic center of the city in a beautifully refurbished old building and is open from Monday to Saturday from 6:30 a.m. until 3 p.m. You can buy local products, organic food and fresh fish, cheese, and cured meats all under cover. On Saturday mornings, the streets surrounding the market are filled with local crafts and products for sale.

***

The Smartest Way to Shop the Stalls:

- ❖ Arrive early to get the top produce.
- ❖ Don't be afraid to haggle.
- ❖ Take cash with you—many traders don't accept card payments.
- ❖ Take reusable bags (or a rolling shopping caddy).
- ❖ Wander around and explore the entire market before you buy anything to see what is on offer.
- ❖ If there is a queue of locals around a stall, the produce there is probably the freshest.

***

⊚ Olhão

Monkfish dreams come true

The heart of Olhão is the waterfront food market, one of the best in southern Portugal. It is housed in two century-old red-brick market halls. It sells the usual gamut of food in these parts, from chicken to Algarve sea salt, from local honey to fruit and vegetables, but as befits a fishing port, it has an impressive range of fish, including tasty monkfish (*tamboril* in Portuguese) that you don't normally find in supermarkets. The market is open from 7 a.m. until 1 p.m. Monday to Saturday. On Saturdays, it's combined with an open-air market with local handicraft producers selling their goods as well.

***

⚲ Portimão

The Algarve's largest harvest under one roof

The municipal market in Portimão is one of the largest indoor markets in the Algarve. It's an excellent resource with everything you need to eat fresh, locally sourced produce on sale here. As well as fresh fruit, vegetables and fish, you can buy local delicacies and gastronomic products, flowers, and traditional craft items. This is where many of the top restaurants and smaller local markets source their produce. It's open from 7 a.m. to 2 p.m. and again between 5 p.m. to 8 p.m. Monday to Friday and from 7 a.m. to 2 p.m. on Saturdays and holidays.

***

⚲ Quarteira

A mile from town, a world of deals

Quarteira market is one of the most popular in the Algarve and is a great place to pick up a bargain. The market can be found about a mile outside the town on the main road to Almancil, close to the Aquashow waterpark. It's held every week on Wednesdays from 8 a.m. to 3 p.m. They sell everything from clothing to sunglasses, local products, games, toys, and plants, ceramics, shoes, handbags, linens, and cork products.

***

⚲ Tavira

A market where tradition meets trend

Located along the riverside in Tavira, this market combines a traditional-style market with more modern shops. The market is open daily (except Sundays) from 7 a.m. to 3 p.m. when you can buy products, fruit, fish, meat, clothing, and toys. On the first and fourth Saturday of the month, you'll find the antique market here.

***

The Islands

⦿ Madeira

Culture meets craft in Madeira's signature stitches

Renowned for its intricate and high-quality hand-stitched designs, with an abundance of floral motifs, cutwork, scalloped edges, and types of stitches, Madeira's embroidery involves many hours of highly skilled labor and is even regulated by Legal Decree.

It's assumed that the skill was brought to the island by its first settlers, shortly after the island was discovered, in the 15th century. Typically, this embroidery is made on cotton fabric or fine linen and is usually white-on-white, although modern colorful designs can also be found.

National Bests

Colorful, whimsical, and always Portuguese: The power of the rooster

Whether you're in the north or the south of Portugal, looking for rustic or upscale, practical or decorative, you're bound to come across a local kind of ceramic…

Most famous types of local ceramic work include black clay (*barro negro*) in north and Central Portugal, the whimsical designs from Bordalo Pinheiro in Caldas da Rainha, the colorful roosters in Barcelos, the high-end porcelain from Vista Alegre, and the rustically minimalist style of Alentejo's pottery.

Even though some aspects of Portuguese ceramics have adapted to the changing times, many traditional styles have been kept and can still be found. A dish cabinet is not complete without some Portuguese pottery bought from the ceramicist who made it… and you really can't live in Portugal without some representation of the Barcelos rooster someplace in the home!

*****

From Hangman's Noose To National Treasure: The Rooster Myth

Wondering why the rooster is seen all over the country?

The legend goes back to the time of a serial killer reigning terror over the little town of Barcelos in the Minhos province in the 15th century...

A pilgrim came through town on his way to Santiago de Compostela and was blamed for the murders. He was sentenced to hang but demanded to plead his case to a judge in person. He was brought in front of the judge as he tucked into his rooster dinner, which he was promptly put off of and put to the side.

The pilgrim said, "If I am hanged and am innocent, this cooked cock will stand and crow as the noose is dropped."

Of course, this was met with laughter... until it came to pass. The judge promptly rushed out to save the pilgrim.

To this day, the story stands as an allegory to the Portuguese love of life—to perseverance and to never giving up. That your life is worth living even when faced with the toughest challenges...

***

From reeds to riches: The woven wonders of Portugal

In Portugal, basket weaving has existed since pre-Roman times. Traditionally, over the centuries, artisans weaved baskets of all sizes, using reeds, wicker, or straw, for a multitude of daily life purposes. Today, you'll find this sustainable handicraft being used to make not only baskets but also handbags and many contemporary more decorative items, like jewelry cases, placemats, or even mirror frames.

***

Azulejos: The tile that tells a tale

Whether they have simple geometric designs or depict complex religious or historical scenes, wherever you are in Portugal, you're bound to see *azulejos*, Portuguese decorative tiles. Of Moorish origin, *azulejos* saw their moment of glory in Portuguese history right after the 1755 earthquake: rebuilding had to be quick, and covering newly-built walls in *azulejo* not only filled in the aesthetic part but also helped regulate the buildings' temperature and provided insulation. The motifs and production methods have changed with the times, but *azulejo* is still used today, although usually with more minimalistic designs.

***

Portugal's endless cork creations

We've all seen cork stoppers… and if you've ever been to any part of Portugal, you'll have seen cork put to a lot more uses than that…

Thermoses, for example, were created independently by shepherds in Alentejo who used cork containers to keep their food warm.

Harvested from the bark of cork oak trees, cork is a versatile material with unique traits: it's lightweight, naturally water-resistant, heat-resistant, insulating, sustainable, and biodegradable—all of this while having a remarkably smooth texture.

But since the olden days, the Portuguese have really learned to capitalize on ways to creatively use cork. Its use in handicrafts is almost endless, and today, you can find it in many different objects, from jewelry, shoes, and bags to hats and home décor.

***

Portugal's most legendary threads

Some traditional types of fabric have stood the test of time and are still being manufactured in Portugal today, like linen, *burel*, and *chita de Alcobaça*.

Linen is fairly well known but most aren't aware of the incredible amount of work that goes into it. In Portugal, the most remote trace of its growth and use dates back to the Bronze Age (2,000 B.C.), in the Serra de Monchique in the Algarve region. Linen clothing is famous for being light, but artisans today are also using it in hats, shoes, and even jewelry.

Burel is a traditional handcrafted Portuguese fabric, made exclusively from sheep's wool of the Bordaleira, Churra, and Merina breeds. It's found mostly in Central Portugal, where this fabric became a wintertime staple for providing wonderful insulation against the cold, the rain, and the snow (with no pilling, by the way). These days, *burel* is being used mostly to create capes and coats, with designs that go from the traditional to the contemporary.

Chita is a printed cotton fabric (similar to calico) that originates from India, and which was brought to Europe in the 15th century by the Portuguese. Characteristic of *chita de Alcobaça* are the colorful patterns with wide strips, where elements such as animals, flowers, fruits, and cornucopias indicate an Indo-European influence. Even though it's not easy to find it anymore, artisans are still making use of its cheerful patterns to create items like bags or covers for books.

3. Sights And Sites

Portugal is a smorgasbord of things to see and do…

Thanks to its history, this small country packs a strong cultural punch. This part of Iberia has been inhabited by dozens of different cultures, each making a distinctive mark on the country.

From prehistory, to the Lusitanians, the Gallaeci, the Celtici, and the Cynetes… to visits from the Phoenician-Carthaginian world and then into the Roman period… from Germanic and Visigoth invasions, Viking incursions… to Sephardic Jewish settlements and the Moorish Umayyad invasion… from the mass expulsions of the Inquisition and Reconquista periods to the current century, which has seen the country become a cultural and artistic powerhouse in Europe.

Nowadays, museums, music, and the arts of all kinds are ubiquitous—even in the smallest villages, you'll find something of interest to explore not too far.

And, of course, with so many religions passing through over the centuries, religious sites of all kinds can be found across the country.

Northern Portugal

⊘ Porto

Worship in your own words

Porto is home to the international English-speaking church of Saint James (Anglican).

***

The biggest synagogue in the country

The Kadoorie-Mekor Haim synagogue, which is an Orthodox Jewish congregation, is the largest synagogue on the Iberian Peninsula and one of the largest in Europe. In the 1930s, before the building was even complete, the Israeli Technology Institute was installed.

***

From the top of Portugal's tallest tower, Porto awaits

The Clérigos Church Tower in Porto is one of the most emblematic monuments in the city and the highest tower in Portugal at 75 meters, or 240 steps, tall. From the top, you'll enjoy a 360-degree, unparalleled view of the city.

***

Eiffel's forgotten bridge

A somewhat unknown claim to fame, the Ponte D. Maria bridge in Porto was designed by Gustav Eiffel (yes, the same Eiffel that designed and built the Eiffel Tower) and was considered a remarkable feat of engineering at the time.

***

The bridge that got the last laugh

Ponte Dom Luís I (Dom Luís Bridge) is the most iconic bridge in Porto, named a UNESCO World Heritage Site in 1996. Built in the 80s, the metallic structure with two stories connects the cities of Porto and Vila Nova de Gaia, which are separated by the river. The upper story runs a metro line across, while the lower allows for car traffic.

More often referred to simply as the Luís I Bridge, there's a city legend behind this shortened name. According to stories passed from generation to generation, the king wasn't present at the inauguration of the bridge, so the proud Porto people refused to put "Dom" in the name as revenge for the lack of respect he supposedly showed the city. Truth or not, its beauty and grandeur can't be denied...

***

Art space meets botanic garden

Serralves in Porto, is an 18-hectare multiuse space with formal gardens, natural woods, a traditional farmhouse, a contemporary art museum, and more. Considered one of the most important cultural centers in the country, Serralves has received international recognition and was classified as a national monument in 2012.

A center for contemporary art, architecture, and landscape, its mission is to promote the arts to those of all ages, as well as being a repository for arts and research. Enjoy its exhibitions, seasonal markets (where you'll be introduced to fabulous local products and the artisans who created them), and the 8,000+ specimens of notable plants throughout the grounds, representing about 230 species.

*****

Architectural masterpiece or meteorite?

Casa Da Música is Porto's concert hall, conceived to commemorate Porto's 2001 European Capital of Culture win, and is credited with renewing locals' interest in the arts. Right in the heart of the city on Boavista Avenue, its unconventional architectural style gets mixed reactions. Many consider it to be an architectural masterpiece… but some say it looks like a meteorite landed in the middle of the city. With two main auditoriums (holding 1,238 and 300 people, respectively), it also offers a superb view over the city through its rooftop restaurant. As the first building in Portugal exclusively dedicated to music, this monument to the arts is worth a visit.

Perhaps counterintuitively, Casa da Música is not only an icon for music, it's also one of the best places in the city to skate. Its unusual exterior architecture creates ramps, slopes, and bowls that attract skaters from all over the area, along with the wide-open space and the fact that the stone dries quickly after rain.

*****

One-stop shop for culture and performance

The Coliseu Do Porto And The Teatro Municipal Do Porto are the city's theaters offering year-long programs that include national and international symphonies, opera, ballet, plays and a variety of other types of show (like puppetry, circuses, and even movie screenings).

*****

Porto's most breathtaking building: where history meets luxury

The Palácio Da Bolsa is one of the most beautiful buildings in Porto... With a mix of architectural styles, you'll be greeted at the entrance by a granite and marble staircase.

As you walk through, you'll come across the Golden Room, completely wallpapered with gold leaf, stunning ceiling frescoes, sculptures, and much more, all of which lead you to the pièce de resistance: The breathtaking Arab Room, designed entirely in the Moorish Revival style, all finished in wood, stucco, and gold leaf. The Arabic inscriptions and exotic figures on the walls are all hand-painted.

This is where visiting dignitaries are hosted, all important receptions are held, and a popular classical music concert hall is located.

***

Porto's most deliciously diverse cultural complex

The World of Wine in Porto's Wine Quarter houses 7 museums, 12 restaurants, bar and café spaces, a wine school, shops, an exhibition hall, and an event space.

Located in Vila Nova de Gaia, on the south bank of the River Douro, overlooking the Ribeira of Porto (Porto's Riverside) and the Luís I Bridge, the project started with the restoration of old port wine cellars and aims to convey the history and feeling associated with winemaking in its many forms.

There are seven themed museums:

- ❖ The Wine Experience
- ❖ The Porto Region Across the Ages (history and heritage of Porto)
- ❖ Planet Cork
- ❖ The Chocolate Story
- ❖ The Bridge Collection (traces the chronology of the glass as an object)
- ❖ The Porto Fashion and Fabric Museum
- ❖ The Pink Palace, which specializes in rosé wine specifically

For those interested in discovering local wines and culture, this complex is definitely worth your attention.

Central Portugal

⊙ Almada

From friars to fine arts

An hour south of Lisbon, Almada is home to the Capuchos convent. Built in 1558, this former convent of the Order of Saint Francis has adapted part of its premises to host exhibitions and cultural events, from visual arts to classical music. Many know this space for its chapel (where weddings and baptisms are still celebrated to this day) and for its peaceful surroundings, which include a viewpoint from which visitors can enjoy the views of parts of Lisbon, Estoril, and Cascais.

***

Secret faith, enduring spirit

About two hours inland from Coimbra is the little town of Belmonte (part of the district of Castelo Branco), and it's home to the most well-known example of Crypto-Jewish communities in Portugal. The Jewish population here dates to the 13th century, secretly maintaining their traditions despite the Inquisition and forced conversions. Open practice was re-established with a synagogue, founded in 1996, and the Belmonte Jewish Museum, opened in 2005, chronicles the town's remarkable history.

***

⊙ Caldas da Rainha

From royal decree to national treasure

In Caldas da Rainha, Igreja De Nossa Senhora Do Pópulo, meaning "Church of Our Lady of the Populace," is a late Gothic church built around 1500 by order of Queen Leonor. It was declared a national monument in 1910 and features both Mudéjar and Manueline architectural characteristics. Nearby, don't miss the 18th-century fountain, known as Chafariz das 5 Bicas (fountain of the five spouts).

***

Holy spokes! Where two wheels tell stories

The Museu Do Ciclismo (Cycling Museum) in Caldas da Rainha is a small, free-entry museum that brings together a collection of not only bicycles but also photos and other objects that illustrate the history of cycling in Portugal. The Volta a Portugal em Bicicleta (equivalent to the Tour de France or the Vuelta in Spain) had its first edition in 1927, and even though it's still popular today, from the 1950s to the 1970s, this sporting event used to galvanize the country. Even if you're not particularly interested in cycling, it's worth taking some time to explore this exhibition.

***

Brushstrokes of history—the pioneer of Portuguese museums

The José Malhoa Museum, located in the Dom Carlos I Park of Caldas da Rainha, was the first building in Portugal to be designed specifically for museum purposes. Here you'll find the largest collection of works from José Malhoa, a local artist who was also one of Portugal's most acclaimed painters and designers from the late 19th century and early 20th century. He became famous for his naturalistic portrayal of popular Portuguese figures and scenes, and the museum showcases several of his most iconic works, like the painting "The Promises." This museum also includes other wonderful examples of 19th and 20th-century painting, sculpture, and ceramics by artists like Maria Helena Vieira da Silva, Columbano, Rafael Bordalo Pinheiro, and Delfim Maya. A ticket costs 3 euros and gives you a 50% discount on the ticket to the Ceramics Museum (valid for a week).

***

Ceramic capital of Portugal

Caldas da Rainha's Ceramics Museum and Bordallo Pinheiro Factory Shop, offers a collection of ceramics going from the 18th century to present day. This includes, of course, several works by famous Portuguese artist Bordallo Pinheiro. The Bordallo Pinheiro Factory shop was established in 1884, is mostly run by women today, and is a great place to buy pottery, with a massive collection of goods.

***

⊚ Cascais

Craft, culture, and community since 1964

The event space in Monte Estoril, near Cascais, F.I.A.R.T.I.L., is always hopping with some food or wine festival, or seasonal or cultural market. Enjoy performances of popular music, fado, and folklore as you snack on nibbles from local restaurants who come to showcase their specialties. It's most famous for its annual Feira Internacional de Artesanato do Estoril, a craft fair that has been held since 1964.

***

Garden of gatherings

Aside from being a lovely place to spend time outdoors, with lawns, gardens, ponds, wildlife, petting zoo, and more, Cascais' Parque Marechal Carmona is also a summer venue. Hosting several events throughout the year, including music festivals, kids' days, and more—when in Cascais check their event calendar.

***

⊚ Sintra

Where palaces grow on hills—the town that artists and aristocrats built

For centuries, Lisbon saw Sintra as a kind of resort for both the nobles and the bourgeoisie, especially in the summer. For many centuries, the closeness to Lisbon, paired with the hills and forests, made Sintra a favorite of royals and artists alike. The attention and growth it experienced at this time are visible in the villas that still exist and help create its trademark romantic atmosphere. The oldest hotel in the Iberian Peninsula, Lawrence's Hotel, was established in this period, is located in Sintra and is still functioning.

The green landscapes of Sintra seemed to have been tailor-made to accommodate architectural feasts of the Romanticism period, like Monserrate and Pena palace. This appealed not only to Portuguese artists but to foreign ones as well. Lord Byron, Richard Strauss, and Hans Christian Andersen are among those who visited and loved Sintra.

Palaces, chalets, and manors of varying sizes were built throughout the centuries, many of which are still standing. Among the last of the most spectacular such buildings are Quinta da Regaleira and the Biester palace, both of which can be visited. In 1995, Sintra was classified by UNESCO as a Cultural Landscape and World Heritage Site.

⊚ Coimbra

Where Romanesque still reigns

The Sé Velha (Old Cathedral) of Coimbra was constructed following the demolition of a mosque, where the cathedral now stands, during the Reconquista period. The original basilica, dating back to the early 10th century, was destroyed in 1117, but you can see its votive foundation stone inside the present-day cathedral. Its construction began in 1139, funded by Afonso Henriques, Portugal's first king, and unlike many Romanesque cathedrals in the country, this one has remained relatively intact.

In the 16th century, a new Renaissance-style doorway called Porta Especiosa was added. Notable features within include Mudéjar-style tiles (some of the oldest in Portugal) imported from Seville and the Gothic cloister, recognized as Portugal's oldest. The cathedral's interior showcases a flamboyant Gothic main altarpiece crafted between 1498 and 1502 by Flemish artisans Olivier de Ghent and Jean d'Ypres. Additionally, there are well-preserved side altars and Gothic tombs of bishops and saints.

***

Baroque brilliance in Coimbra

Coimbra's New Cathedral (or Sé Nova), built in the 17th century, was originally the church of the Jesuits in Coimbra. After the Jesuit order was banned from the country, the seat of the bishop was moved from the old cathedral (Sé Velha) to this newer and much larger one, which then became the New Cathedral. Especially relevant are the two Baroque altars covered in gold leaf, the 18th-century organs, and the Manueline-style baptismal font.

***

Where Renaissance meets Moorish magic

Jardim Da Manga, next to Coimbra's church of Santa Cruz, is one of the most Instagram-worthy places in the city. Featuring a central dome-shaped structure, which rests on eight columns and is surrounded by four small chapels, this courtyard of sorts used to be one of the cloisters of the Santa Cruz monastery. Dating back to the 15th century, Jardim da Manga is one of the first Portuguese architectural works entirely Renaissance in style. At the same time, its structure is reminiscent of the Fountain of Life and greatly inspired by Arabic architecture and its fountains.

***

Walk in the footsteps of an assassin

Santa Clara-a-Velha (the Old Santa Clara) is an abandoned medieval monastery on the banks of the Mondego River, originally built in the 14th century. Only ruins remain today, but it is one of the most complete and historically important Gothic ruins in Portugal.

Famously, it's the place where the problematic Inês de Castro was assassinated by the King of Portugal. Having arranged the marriage of his son the prince, he was galled to find the prince had fallen in love with his fiancé's cousin, Ines de Castro, and kept her as his mistress. When the prince's wife died, he refused to marry anyone but Ines. The king had her killed in the monastery… but the love story doesn't end there.

Once the prince ascended to the throne, legend has it that he tracked down her killers and had their hearts ripped out. He then exhumed Ines and had her coronated, dressed in full regalia, and demanded his court swear her allegiance. They are now buried alongside each other not far from this site.

Sometimes called the Romeo and Juliet of Portugal, this tragic, grisly story is one of the most well-known in Portugal and has been the inspiration for countless works of art and drama.

***

Sanctuary of the saint queen

Coimbra's Santa Clara-a-Nova (the New Santa Clara) is a convent founded in the 17th century, famous for housing the tomb of Saint Queen Elizabeth, the patron saint of Coimbra and a beloved figure in Portugal. Devoted to the poor and by all accounts an incredibly compassionate person, she cared for the sick, the orphaned, the homeless, and the local religious orders, providing them housing and support—even without the support of her husband, the king.

***

Birthplace of books, tomb of kings

Igreja De Santa Cruz in Coimbra was established in 1131 and rebuilt in the 16th century. It was originally a monastery and a prominent hub for national and international theological studies during the early stages of the nation's formation.

Renowned for its library and scriptorium, where monks copied books, this church holds immense historical significance. Plus, this is where you'll find the tombs of Portugal's first two kings, Afonso Henriques and his son Sancho I. If you like exploring nooks and crannies in historical buildings, buy the ticket that allows you access to the sacristy, the cloister, the Chapter House, and several other spaces.

Right next to this church, you'll see Café Santa Cruz, an iconic space in the city of Coimbra. Even though this has been a café since 1923, the original building was actually an auxiliary chapel to the church.

***

Where Roman foundations meet baroque grandeur

Coimbra's Machado de Castro National Museum is a must-see. Aside from its impressive selection of art, the building itself is a piece of living history, as the foundations are the remains of a Roman forum (and yes, you can visit them). Modern architectural elements were added to a Baroque-style building from the second half of the 18th century (that used to be the Bishop's palace). Named after the acclaimed Portuguese sculptor Joaquim Machado de Castro (1731 to 1822), in this museum you can appreciate Greek, Roman, and Romanesque sculptures as well as 13th-century Islamic ceramics, 16th-century paintings, and 18th-century furniture, among other features.

The 1st-century cryptoporticus is an underground gallery, built to support the forum that existed at the time while also compensating for the natural uphill of the terrain.

If you don't have the time to visit any of the exhibitions, do at least take a couple of minutes to appreciate the view from the terrace, which offers stunning panoramas of the old town, including the city's rooftops, the old cathedral, and the Mondego River. That's also where you'll find the museum's café (with outdoor seating) and restaurant, which offers a lunch buffet.

*****

A UNESCO university still making history... where bats patrol the stacks

The University of Coimbra and the Joanina Library are nestled high above the cityscape of Coimbra, in the heart of the old part of the city.

Coimbra University, established in 1290, stands as one of Europe's most ancient and prestigious academic institutions. Because of its legacy, spanning over seven centuries, it holds the distinction of being one of the few universities recognized as a UNESCO World Heritage Site. While the university (as an institution) was founded in Lisbon in 1290, it made Coimbra its permanent physical home in 1537. Despite predating even Oxford University, it remains a thriving, fully functioning institution. You can visit several of the university's buildings with the purchase of a ticket.

The Paço das Escolas, which you enter after passing the solemn-looking "iron door" (Porta Férrea), is a square of sorts that houses the historical nucleus of the university. Originally, it was a fortified palace where the governor lived (during Moorish rule) and was later inhabited by King Afonso Henriques. (Trivia tidbit: almost all of the kings of Portugal's first dynasty were born here.)

The most famous element of this historical nucleus is the Joanina Library, and you have the option to purchase your ticket with or without the library included. Bear in mind that the library visit is timed, and when you buy your ticket, you will be allocated a time slot (no exceptions allowed). Buy online ahead of time to avoid arriving on site and it being sold out (employees say tickets are usually gone for the day by 1 or 2 p.m.).

The Joanina Library, also known as the Baroque Library, is probably the most spectacular feature of the university. This Baroque gem was built between 1717 and 1728 during the reign and by order of King Dom João V and has around 60,000 volumes, from the 16th to the 18th centuries. If you can, try to go there when there is more natural light, as the gold leaf covering the bookshelves and decorations will really shine through. Make sure you don't miss the ceilings painted using the trompe l'oeil technique, which creates an impressive perspective.

Before a group enters the library, a guide will announce the opening of the doors, and each group can only stay for 10 minutes—the doors are kept shut to keep the humidity out. Filming or photographing inside are not allowed.

Oh, and book-loving insects, like moths? There is a small colony of bats living in the library, that feeds on them. Talk about eco-friendly solutions!

Other relevant buildings that you can visit include the Grand Hall, the Science Museum (and the Cabinet of Curiosities), the 18th-century clock tower, and Saint Michael's Chapel. The present-day chapel is the consequence of the 16th-century rebuilding of the previous one, probably dating from the 11th century. The frescos make for a spectacular view, and don't miss the organ, built in 1733.

* * *

⦿ Lisbon

A Rembrandt, a rose garden, and a really rich Armenian

The Calouste Gulbenkian Museum in Lisbon, which houses the personal art collection of the man once considered to be the richest in the world thanks to his 5% stake in most of the Middle East's oil fields, is a wonderful place to spend a day. Gulbenkian collected pre-Revolutionary Louis XIV to XVI furniture, gold coins, oriental carpets, and two Rembrandts. Because he left so much money to Portugal, Gulbenkian also financed a modern art collection built up by curators after the Salazar regime Gulbenkian favored had collapsed. The museum collection is varied and spans centuries, and it's located in a sprawling park, the iconic

Gulbenkian Garden, covering an area of around 22 acres (9,000 square meters), one of the most beloved in the city.

*****

⊚ Óbidos

The church that time rebuilt

Igreja De Santa Maria of Óbidos is the main religious building in the town. The exact date of its foundation is uncertain, but we know it has been a church since the 12th century, that previously it had been a mosque (during the time of the Moorish occupation), and that, probably, it had been a Visigoth church before that. The paintings that decorate it (including one from Josefa d'Óbidos) and the decorative tiles that cover the walls are particularly stunning.

*****

A free gem for art lovers

Take some time to visit the small (free) Municipal Museum. Here you'll find paintings and sculptures, mostly religious in nature, and with a big focus on the 16th and 17th centuries. The emphasis is on the works by Portuguese painter, Josefa d'Óbidos.

*****

A medieval fortress turned boutique hotel

The castle of Óbidos is one of the most paradigmatic in the country. The original fortification was likely a pre-Roman *castro*, which would be increasingly amplified throughout the centuries. The 1755 earthquake caused a great deal of damage to the castle and by the 20th century, it was in ruins.

It was restored in the 1930s and the first to become a hotel of the "Pousadas de Portugal," a series of historical buildings (like castles, monasteries, and palaces) that were adapted to become luxury lodgings.

The castle walls can be visited for free and welcome several events throughout the year, with the medieval fair (in July) being one of the most famous. You can walk along the castle walls, but note that some parts are not particularly safe, nor advised for people with vertigo.

***

⊙ Setúbal

Cannons, kings, and killer views

In Setúbal, don't miss the Fort of São Filipe, a fortress overlooking the city on the north bank of the Sado River.

***

═══════ Southern Portugal ═══════

⊙ Faro

Ancient baths, hidden paths

Near the beaches of Faro, you'll find the ruins of the Roman baths dating from the 3rd to 5th century behind a wall that runs alongside the coastal promenade. There is a small sign and a door in the wall, which is easy to miss as you walk along. You'll also see the remnants of a small Roman Aqueduct halfway down the Rua do Poco, set in a small, landscaped garden.

***

⊙ Ferragudo

The Algarve's most unreachable dream home

By 1896, the Ferragudo's fort had been abandoned, lying in ruin until the beginning of the 20th century when the poet, Coelho Carvalho, turned it into a home. It's still privately owned, so you can't go inside, but it's a magnificent landmark jutting out on the headland.

***

⦿ Silves

One of the Algarve's last true gothic churches

The Cathedral of Silves is one of the Algarve's few remaining gothic monuments, and entrance is only 1.50 euro. Originally built in the 13th century, with 15th and 16th century additions and post-earthquake 18th century repairs, the exterior is a mix of whitewashed walls and red sandstone, and the interior is a mix of gothic, medieval, and baroque traditions. The building has an immense sense of height and space, with religious music playing quietly in the background. It feels like a place of worship in the present day as well as a historical record of the past. It's a peaceful place and unusually without much of the gold trappings of many local churches.

***

Where past and paintings collide

Santa Misericórdia Church, located opposite the Silves cathedral, boasts a magnificent Manueline-style door, which is set halfway up the outside wall of the building. If you stepped out of it by mistake, you'd have quite a shock. The church is originally from the 16th century and still has a beautifully painted altarpiece of Our Lady of Mercy visible on the walls. The building is now used as an art gallery, although it's often closed.

***

Silves' underground star

To learn about Silves' history, head to the Archeology Museum, which is built around the Poço-Cisterna Almóada, a 12th century well that was discovered after excavations in the 18th century. The well is now classified as a National Monument and forms the centerpiece of the museum.

***

From swords to stories: Silves' fortress tower library

The turret of one of the main City Gates of Silves, the Torreão da Porta da Cidade, is the only one of the four archways to the *almedina* old town that stands today, and it's an impressive sight, hinting at the fortress-like protection once afforded to the occupants of the city. It's a tall structure, creating images of biblical-sized enemies and soldiers attacking each other. Standing underneath the arch, you feel dwarfed. Today it has the more genteel purpose of housing the municipal library.

***

Portugal's most beautiful death-defying view

Silves Castle, the best-preserved castle in the Algarve, is believed to have been situated on top of Roman fortifications from the 4th or 5th century and was built on the site of the Palace of the Verandhas, whose construction started around 715 by the Moorish occupants.

It's an impressive site, with 11 square towers and red sandstone walls which enclose an area of 12,000 square meters. Some of the towers have gothic doorways, and there are some small exhibition rooms housing artefacts and displays.

The central area has a well-tended garden area with trees and seating. There are also two Roman cisterns. The larger one is called El Moura Encantada ("The Enchanted Moura"), after a legend that says you can hear a Moorish princess mourning her beloved at the well where he committed suicide. You can view this cistern underground through the clear walkways.

The view from the top is stunning, with panoramic views across the city and surrounding countryside, although the walkways are not for the fainthearted or young. In many places, there are no railings, and there's quite a drop. It's well worth a trip up to the castle if you don't mind the climb. The views across Silves and the neighboring countryside more than make up for it. Watch out if it has been raining, as the combination of worn smooth *calçada* stones and wet weather can be lethal.

***

⦿ **Tavira**

Ancient tech for a sharp view

A camera obscura, installed in an old water tower of Tavira, gives you an unparalleled overview of the city. Using an optical system of mirror and lenses, a 360-degree view of the settlement is projected onto a surface in a darkened room. The attraction's guide, originally from London but a long-time Algarve resident, holds forth on Tavira's history, starting with the salt-pans on the edge of town that have been worked for at least 2,500 years.

***

The most haunted fortress in Portugal

Tavira's castle, begun by the Moors in the 10th century on the site of a Phoenician temple complex. Today it has a most unmilitary vibe, with bougainvillea climbing the walls up to the height of the battlements and plants from Brazil helping to create a colorful, exotic garden.

Local legend tells of a "Moira," the spirit of a Moorish woman who on Saint John's Eve every year (June 23) appears in the castle to mourn her destiny. The daughter of the Moorish governor at the time, the town was then conquered by Christians, and the governor is said to have disappeared by magic after enchanting his daughter. He planned to retake the city and rescue her… but never succeeded.

In another episode, the ghosts of seven knights who died protecting the castle and were then named protectors of the city appeared to a would-be conqueror, driving him away and thus saving the town a second time.

***

A convent, a cappuccino, and the caliphate

Tavira's Pousada Convento, a hotel set in a 16th-century former convent houses some Islamic ruins that most don't get to see. Drop in for a coffee in the bar and then ask to see the 13th century Islamic ruins, which are down some stairs in a yard at the back. Bar staff have the key.

***

⊚ Praia da Luz

The Algarve's most creative corner for all ages

The Luz Cultura art project brings together art, music, and creative souls under one roof in Praia da Luz. The venue hosts music lessons, a choir, art workshops, keep fit and dance classes, and a summer school for children. They even have Portuguese language classes and music sessions for babies and toddlers (and their parents). The venue regularly hosts art exhibitions by local artists.

***

Where cannons once boomed, guitars now strum

Fortaleza da Luz or Castelo da Senhora da Luz dates back to around 1640, created to defend the region against pirates and invasions—originally with 5-meter-tall walls, they must have been expecting trouble. Today, it's a far more genteel place, with a restaurant and bar and live music on Sunday afternoons. It's lovely to walk past and hear their music wafting out from inside the gardens.

***

4. *Festas!* (Festivals)

One of the most vibrant aspects of Portuguese traditions is the *festa*. Literally translating to party, really, the term covers a wide scope of events that are significant in Portuguese culture.

Festas take place in every town in Portugal, big or small, and can be linked to local patron saints, historical dates, medieval and Renaissance fairs, food festivals, or any significant cultural attraction.

Most festivals take place between late May and mid-September. It's elementary math: warm weather = *festas*.

Even though each *festa* shows a different side to the heart of Portuguese culture, there are many common aspects. They're the perfect opportunity to immerse oneself in the traditional Portuguese festive spirit.

Best of all, they're free and open to all.

Of course, many of these events are raucous, with loudspeakers blasting music, fireworks at all hours, kids throwing firecrackers at your feet, water being thrown from all sides… and some of the more odd traditions, like being hit on the head with a plastic hammer or being pelted with flour…

If this doesn't sound like the kind of atmosphere you'd enjoy, the best thing to do is avoid being in town for a *festa*. That in mind, think of this as either a guide to enjoying the *festas* or avoiding them!

As you plan your trip to Portugal or think about exploring more of your new home country, you might want to include one or two *festas* in your itinerary. So pack your bags, bring your appetite, and get ready to dive into the world of Portuguese *festas*!

Northern Portugal

⦿ Aveiro

A splash of pride in the city of canals

June: Aveiro has for some years now organized a Pride Parade in June (Marcha do Orgulho LGBTQ+ de Aveiro) with a march that crosses the town. While you'll see plenty of pride, rainbows, and a few drag queens, this march is fairly conservative compared to what you might be used to in bigger cities.

***

⦾ **Braga**

Easter at its most reverent

March/April: In Braga, Holy Week is lived as a great and solemn event. Celebrations here date to the 4th century and are some of Portugal's most famous. Every night, processions follow various routes through the center of town, with people walking the streets carrying images of Christ and stopping for prayers and hymns in several churches. There are also several events hosted around the themes of Lent, Easter, and Holy Week, such as classical music concerts and exhibitions.

***

Travel back to Roman times

May: Emperor Caesar Augustus founded three cities in the north-west of Hispania, one of which was Bracara Augusta, now called Braga. In the 4th century, it even became the capital of the Gallician province. To celebrate this illustrious past, Bracara Romana is held every year. The city recreates its Roman past, complete with a Roman fort, food and wine stalls, merchandise, musicians, dancers… and even Roman chariot races. For five days in May, the city and all its inhabitants and visitors dress up for the occasion—don't be caught without a costume!

***

Nine days of sardines and street dancing

June: Braga celebrates São João (Saint John) in June with a nine-day festival that ends on June 24. There's lots of entertainment, parades, street dancing, concerts, a fair, and lots of grilled sardines, plus red wine.

***

A city-wide white party

September: The first week of September is when Braga delivers its largest festival of the year—Noite Branca, or "White Night." Everyone wears white clothing, and stages are erected on most street corners, as well as in public squares and municipal gardens. Live bands, DJs, and other musical acts perform through the night, with new acts every hour. Thousands of people come to dance the night away... On the last of the three nights, an estimated two million people show up bedecked in white and ready to dance.

***

The world's most civilized pub crawl

September: In September, a month-long restaurant festival called Verde Cool has each restaurant in town featuring a regional pairing of a glass of vinho verde with a *petisco* (Portugal's version of tapas) for just 3 euros. It's like a civilized, city-wide pub crawl.

***

A very Braga Christmas

December: Don't miss the quirky Braga Christmas Eve tradition of drinking *muscatel* wine and eating bananas at Casa das Bananas in Braga. Manuel Rio started the tradition a few decades ago at his banana warehouse near the center of town.

***

⊚ Canas de Senhorim

The most contentious carnival

February: A truly unique *carnival* has been born from a rivalry lasting over 400 years between two neighborhoods of Canas de Senhorim in the Viseu district, about an hour inland from Aveiro.

The Paço neighborhood was the upscale area, and the Rossio neighborhood was the impoverished area—*carnival* provided the ideal background for complaints and criticisms in a relaxed environment. Each neighborhood marches with its own parade, and, in the end, the neighborhood that shows the most energy and joy wins.

Monday includes the *Farinhada* (from *farinha*, meaning flour), in which girls run the risk of being heavily dusted with flour before noon and older women after noon.

On Ash Wednesday, after a community dinner, Shrovetide (in the form of a doll) is taken through the streets and burned in public.

***

⦿ **Estarreja**

The samba carnival

February: The *carnival* of Estarreja first appeared in the local press in 1903, with news about a lively Battle of Flowers parade. This was not a battle per se, but rather the decoration of windows and balconies, as well as a parade.

In the 1980s, samba became part of the *carnival* celebrations. Nowadays, in addition to the *corsos*, Estarreja hosts the National Samba Trophy, a competition bringing together the samba schools that won the *carnivals* across the country.

***

⦿ **Lazarim**

A boy-versus-girl carnival

February: Lazarim *carnival* focuses on the verbal confrontation between two social groups, the *comadres* and *compadres* (respectively, girls and boys), who meet on Shrove Tuesday, starring in a comical procession rife with social criticism.

In the end, the dolls representing both groups are burned, and everything ends in a party, with food and drink. Typical of Lazarim are the masks made of alder wood and often decorated with horns.

***

⦿ **Ovar**

The most community-based carnival

February: Organized since 1952, the Ovar *carnival* attracts thousands of visitors every year. The festivities are organized entirely by volunteers from the municipality, with more than 2,000 dancers, most of them locals from Ovar.

The main events are the three *carnival corsos* (parades) and the "Magic Night," an event that brings together thousands of partygoers in the city center in a street party that lasts until dawn.

While in other locations the *carnival* king and queen are public figures (like actors or musicians), in Ovar it is local citizens who are chosen. This is a simple yet meaningful way to recognize and appreciate their contribution and involvement in the community.

***

⊚ Podence

The oldest carnival celebration

February: The *carnival* celebrations of Podence are one of the most important events in the north of the country, and they're presumed to have pre-Roman roots.

In Podence, the stars of the show are masked characters called *caretos*, which in 2019 were classified by UNESCO as Intangible Heritage of Humanity. *Caretos* wear colorful woolen suits with rattles at the waist and red, yellow, and green fringes. Their faces are covered by masks made of leather, brass, or wood, and they carry staffs.

On Tuesday and Sunday, the *caretos* take to the streets, dancing, running, and jumping, teasing and taunting visitors and young women in particular.

Originally, *caretos* were boys and young men. However, due to the desertification that started mostly in the 1960s, the recovery of this tradition was only possible when women also started wearing colorful suits.

***

⊚ Porto

The festival to be hit on the head and burn your feet

June: The festival not to miss in Porto is the annual Saint John's festival, a mix of Christian and pre-Christian traditions. In this case, you have a religious celebration dedicated to Saint John the Baptist that takes place in midsummer and includes jumping over bonfires. On the evening of June 23, the streets of Porto are flooded with people from the city and surrounding areas, ready to eat, drink, and dance until the next day. Expect strangers to hit you on the head with leek flowers and soft plastic hammers. At midnight, the sky lights up with an epic display of fireworks.

***

⦾ Vinhais

Where all hell breaks loose for carnival

February: At the tippy top of the country, the town of Vinhais puts an emphasis on devils for *carnival*. On Ash Wednesday, dozens of people dress up as red devils to chase and torment bystanders, especially (you probably guessed it by now) young women.

These devils go through town, following around death, wearing black, and performing mock rituals, sometimes with some malice thrown in.

This event gathers around a thousand people dressed as red devils parading in the streets, although it also includes several other performances.

***

How To *Festa* Like A Local

Each *festa* shows a different side to the heart of Portuguese culture, but there are many shared traits: they happen mostly in open spaces, they're fun, and they're loud!

❖ **Music & Dancing:** Some are traditional, like ranchos *folclóricos* (folk dance groups), while others are what we call *pimba* music. *Pimba* is a type of popular Portuguese music that uses catchy tunes, easy-to-dance rhythms, puns, and, quite often, sexual innuendos. You'll still see grannies dancing to it, though.

❖ **Religious Processions:** Many *festas* are in honor of saints, so expect some kind of religious celebration (like a mass or a procession, at least) as well as flower carpets in some locations.

❖ **Street Decorations:** Streets are decked out in colorful paper garlands, lights, flowers, and themed decorations. *Manjerico*, a type of basil, is commonly sold in little pots in June.

❖ **Fireworks & Parades:** Many *festas*, big and small, will include fireworks and, in some cases, a parade that includes a brass band.

❖ **Street Food & Drinks:** Common foods include grilled sardines, *bifanas*, and *farturas*, along with beer and sangria (more on that further ahead).

To appreciate Portugal's *festas* and have the best possible experience, there are a few important things to keep in mind:

1. **Savor the Local Cuisine:** The food is without a doubt among the highlights of any *festa*. Obviously, there are food trends, but the classics are always there for you.

   You can count on stalls grilling sardines (*sardinhas*) and mackerel (*carapaus*)—a Portuguese summer classic—often served with a slice of bread, roasted bell pepper salad, and boiled potatoes. Grilled sardines and mackerel are typically seasoned with only sea salt and then grilled over hot coals.

   For those who prefer meat, *bifanas* (slices of marinated pork served in a bread roll) are a tasty alternative. Historical fairs will often have stalls slow-roasting entire pigs.

   Vegan and vegetarian options, although increasingly common, are still easier to find in cities and bigger towns.

2. **Drink Responsibly:** Wine, sangria, and beer (including craft beer) are the beverages of choice at *festas*. Especially in urban areas, caipirinhas have become a sort of

modern classic.

When visiting historical fairs, trying mead is a must. Look for signs saying *hidromel.*

3. **Indulge in Sweet Treats:** Make sure to leave room for dessert, as no *festa* is complete without churros and *farturas.* The dough is similar for both, and they're both deep-fried, but they're not the same.

4. **Prepare for Cash Transactions:** While many stalls accept digital payments like MBWay, bringing coins and small bills (5, 10, and 20 euros) can make things easier for everyone, especially when it comes to food and drinks.

5. **Dress Comfortably:** Festivals involve a lot of standing and walking, so comfortable shoes are a must. You'll want to enjoy the party without worrying about sore feet. And don't even think about wearing anything fancy: those who truly live the *festas* will inevitably be going back home smelling of barbecue smoke and with a stain of sangria on their shirts. So relax and just dress casually and comfortably.

6. **Transportation:** Since many *festas* take place in historical centers, it's wise to plan your transportation accordingly. Especially in the case of cities, usually your best option is to park near public transportation and then take the metro or bus. In most smaller towns, there will typically be at least one parking area near the festival—and it will fill up quickly.

7. **Embrace the Atmosphere:** It's likely the festivals in your home country are quite different from the ones in Portugal. Whether you like them or not, it's important to be respectful of the places and people you're visiting. Live and let live—and enjoy the *festa!*

***

Central Portugal

⦿ Almada

Shake it like it's 1599

June: Saint John's festival in Almada, south of Lisbon, offers the traditional street parties, but also *marchas populares*, a traditional form of Portuguese folk music and dance associated with these festivals. *Marchas* involve large groups of participants from different neighborhoods in a friendly kind of competition that revolves around music and dance routines that include local historical and cultural references.

***

⦿ Cascais

Portugal's original jazz fest

July: The Cascais jazz festival, now called Ageas Cooljazz, has been held since 1971 and was the first jazz festival ever held in Portugal. For its inaugural lineup, it welcomed Miles Davis, Dexter Gordon, Phil Woods, and The Giants of Jazz: Thelonious Monk, Kai Winding, Art Blakey, Sonny Stitt, Al McKibbon, and Dizzy Gillespie. It still puts on a hit show that packs a stadium every year with hit artists like Chaka Khan, Diana Krall, and Seal all headlining in recent years.

***

The brightest event in the country

September: For three nights, the LUMINA Light Festival brings light artists from around the world project their art onto city structures and was named as one of the top 10 light festivals in Europe by *The Guardian*. Put on for free, the city promises sculptural, interactive, and immersive works, along with live performances.

***

Yuletide, Portuguese-style

December: Cascais Christmas Village brings Christmas to Cascais each year, with ice rink, giant tree, a live nativity, reindeer, elves, Roman soldiers, the Three Wise Men, and Santa Claus himself. With food vendors, craft stalls, and entertainment spread across Marechal Carmona Park, the whole family can spend hours exploring the grounds and enjoying the activities.

*****

⌖ **Coimbra**

A convent for choreography

April: Since 2003, the Festival Abril Dança em Coimbra has been hosting a dance program that welcomes the whole family. Seminars, workshops, performances, and other events hosted in the spectacular settings of the Convento São Francisco and the Teatro Académico de Gil Vicente.

*****

Watch students burn their garb

May: In Coimbra, "the city of students," the Queima das Fitas (literally, "Burning of the Ribbons") is held every year in May, officially spanning a total of eight days, with parades, concerts, and lots of loud, lively fun. Although it's now held in other university towns and cities, it originated in Coimbra in 1850. Celebrating the end of graduate courses, things can and will get loud and wild. Aside from the students going crazy, thousands of family members, friends, and tourists come to witness this event—if you prefer to avoid this atmosphere, plan to be out of town for this week.

*****

Student voices, ancient stones, timeless song

May: The Serenata Monumental, a Coimbra fado serenade sung by students, is one of the most anticipated events of the year. It takes place on the stairs of the Sé Velha (Old Cathedral). It's an emotional event, so prepare to see people crying, whether or not they're students.

*****

A carnival that connects lost villages

February: In *Góis*, about 45 minutes inland from Coimbra, an almost lost *carnival* tradition was revived, the "race of the Shrovetide." This is not a normal race but rather a route that includes several schist villages in the area.

The goal? To bring back to the depopulated villages the spirit of *carnival* that used to bring together and energize these communities.

Costumes must include cork masks and clothes that are no longer used—the older, the better. Women dress as men, and men dress as women, so that no one knows who is doing all the mischief.

Once the tour is complete, lunch follows, and in the afternoon, there are the usual activities, such as dancing to the sound of *concertinas* (a small type of accordion) and the recitation of rhymes, among others.

Throughout the year, anecdotes involving the inhabitants of these villages are collected and used for these rhymes. They can be said or sung to the sound of *concertinas* or other poorly played instruments—the idea is to make noise.

***

⊘ Lisbon

The carnival of clumsy kings

February: Although *carnival* has been celebrated in Loures, a municipality of Lisbon, to some extent since the early 20th century, 1934 is the year when it officially began. However, there were several interruptions over the years, until the 21st century. Today, the festivities attract tens of thousands of people to the city every year.

This *carnival* event boasts over 2,600 dancers and 15 floats in its parade, plus concerts, nighttime entertainment, and lots of balls (dances). The so-called *Baile Trapalhão* (literally, Clumsy Ball) is famous here—everyone wears the most ridiculous mask they can find. And it all comes to an end with the satirical *Enterro do Rei do Carnival* (Burial of the King of Carnival).

***

Lisbon loud and proud

June: Lisbon hosts the annual Arraial Lisbon Pride event over about two weeks every year, with parades, concerts, games, talks, dancing, and lots of entertainment going late into the night. It's often called the biggest and most colorful celebration in the city, and it's certainly the biggest pride event in the country, going strong since 1997.

***

The ultimate Lisbon festival

June: The quintessential Lisbon festival is Saint Anthony's on June 12 and 13. That's when the streets in the old neighborhoods are at their most colorful with decorations, music, and food. Although this is a religious festival in its origin, it also has a mundane side to it. On the 12th people fill the streets with music playing, dancing, and singing. Expect Portuguese summer classics like sangria, grilled sardines, and *bifanas*. The 13th is for religious celebrations, including the famous "marriages of St Anthony" (and also for curing hangovers from the night before).

***

The only queer film fest in Portugal

September: The Queer Lisboa Film Festival has also been held since 1997, making it the longest running film festival in Lisbon. It's the only event in Portugal that exclusively screens films about gay, lesbian, bisexual, transgender, transsexual, intersex, and other non-normative sexualities and identities, in a genre coined internationally as "Queer Cinema" that is becoming more prevalent in international cinema each year.

***

The biggest Christmas market in Portugal

December: Wonderland Lisboa is one of two of the capital's main Christmas markets and claims to be the biggest in the country. The festival fills Parque Eduardo VII—both literally and figuratively—with holiday cheer. Expect the typical handicrafts and local goods, as well as lots of food trucks. The giant Ferris wheel is a main attraction, offering panoramic views of Lisbon, as is the giant, 800-square-meter skating rink. Kids flock to Santa's village, where they can meet the jolly man himself.

***

⦿ Óbidos

Portugal's most iconic Easter celebration

March/April: In Óbidos, Holy Week attracts thousands of people every year, both Portuguese and foreign. This historical town hosts one of the most impressive and well-known Easter celebrations of its kind in Portugal, which includes the recreation of the last moments of Christ's life on the Stations of the Cross. This procession is one of the oldest in the country, dating back 400 years. In addition to the religious events, there is also a cultural program with classical music concerts.

***

A chocoholic's dream

March/April/May: The Chocolate Festival is one of the country's newest and most popular festivals. For a week each spring, the city is turned into the premier chocolate city in the world. Each year is themed, giving rise to some incredible and creative chocolate sculptures submitted from dozens of participants from around the world showing off their skills. Participate in tastings and workshops with the town castle as the backdrop.

***

The ultimate journey to the Middle Ages

July: For 10 days in July every year, Óbidos is transformed for its Medieval Fair, which will have you absorbed in a living museum populated by hundreds of actors posing as noblemen, beggars, mule-drivers, jugglers, musicians, jesters, dancers, and more.

The town's castle and surrounding walls are the perfect backdrop for this roleplay, which will also feature jousting tournaments, medieval dinners, and a market, where you'll find medieval costumes and accessories as well as things like traditional homemade medical remedies. The food stalls offer authentic Middle Ages fare and serve it in clay dishes, and weapons and tools are displayed and demonstrated. Animals will also be on display, including horses, donkeys, falcons, and snakes.

***

Portugal's winter wonderland

December: Each holiday season, Óbidos turns itself into a kind of enchanted Christmas village called Vila Natal. As well as being an open-air Christmas market, there's a full events program with shows, interactive experiences, and concerts that are fun for the whole family.

***

⊙ **Setúbal**

The ultimate samba festival this side of Rio

July: Sesimbra, a charming town on the coast near Setúbal, welcomes thousands of visitors each July to come to watch the famous samba parades. The MegaSamba festival has become a key samba event in Europe, and it becomes more international every year, uniting composers, singer-songwriters, percussionists, choreographers, dancers, Mestre-sala and Porta-bandeira couples, as well as other representatives of schools of samba from different parts of the world.

***

Portugal's 400-year-old summer bash

July/August: If you're in the region in late July or early August, you need to stop by the Feira de Santiago, without a doubt the most iconic festival in Setúbal. This fair, which is over 400 years old, attracts thousands of people every year and is a smorgasbord of entertainment for the crowds with music, food, sports activities, and handicrafts, among other things. It's one of the largest festivals in this part of Portugal.

***

⊙ **Sintra**

A historic dash to Europe's western edge

January: The Fim da Europa race in January is famous for its scenic beauty, this race starts in Sintra's historical center and ends in Cabo da Roca.

***

Lisbon's most elegant music escape

June: The Sintra Festival, going strong since 1957, focuses on classical music and for the occasion the city opens the doors of its centuries-old palaces and manor houses, as well as using their gardens. For 10 days, enjoy a full calendar of choral and piano recitals and concerts held in some of the city's most spectacular buildings.

***

Where Saint Peter meets street party

June: Sintra commemorates Saint Peter on the 29th (this day is also a municipal holiday). Despite being a religious celebration in its origin, the street partying is quite secular: like its counterparts, Saint Peter's includes live music, dancing, grilled sardines, *bifanas*, and sangria, all in abundance.

***

⊘ Torres Vedras

The carnival capital of the Silver Coast

February: *Carnival* in Torres Vedras, about an hour north of Lisbon, is known for the spontaneous and massive participation of its citizens, as well as for lasting six days.

The first official edition of this *carnival* dates back to 1923, and every year this town on the Silver Coast receives countless visitors dressed up to take part in the parades and watch the *corsos*.

If you know someone from Torres Vedras, it's almost certain that they love *carnival* and live this date intensely. Even the children have a parade of their own, on Friday, where they wear elaborate masks that were made in the schools.

The *corsos* include floats, parade groups, and several mandatory characters, like the *cabeçudos*, accompanied by the *Zés-Pereiras*, and the *matrafonas*.

The *matrafonas* are men disguised as women who started being part of the festivities in 1926. They are meant to be comical, and they often have a clumsy gait.

In Torres Vedras, the King and Queen of *carnival* are always two men, one of whom is dressed as a woman.

Southern Portugal

Oranges and altars: a southern spin on the nativity

December: In the Algarve, instead of the common Nativity scene, some people still decorate in the local traditional way, with a ceramic figurine representing Baby Jesus standing alone on top of a small altar of sorts, covered with a white cloth, and decorated with... oranges!

***

⦿ Alta Mora

A nutty celebration

February: In early February, the inland village of Alta Mora in the eastern Algarve hosts the Almond Blossom Festival, with music, street theater, markets, and hikes through the countryside. It is the time of year when white and pink almond blossoms lend extra charm to the Algarve countryside.

***

⦿ Castelo de Vide

Where Easter belongs to the sheep

March/April: In Castelo de Vide, about two hours inland from Caldas da Rainha, right on the Spanish border, many take to the streets at night, after the Easter Vigil, with rattles and bells.

During the day, parades and processions are held, and the Blessing of the Lambs, an event that used to fill the town with flocks of sheep, also takes place here. Today, there are still some shepherds who take a few of their sheep to the town center to be blessed by the local priest.

***

⦿ Lagoa

The most famous concert in the country

December: Lagoa is known for its annual Christmas concert, which features the amazingly talented singer, Carla Pontes. Offered for free every year in an old and beautiful church in the region for the last 25 years, the concert is always sold out.

***

⊚ Loulé

Algarve's wildest winter party

February: Loulé in Algarve offers the biggest and best *carnival* event in the region, as well as the most exotic expression of it, complete with nearly naked women on floats. It is the oldest in Portugal, totaling over 100 years of continuous celebrations. The stores are flooded with outfits and wigs starting early February. Make sure to arrive early if you plan to celebrate in Loulé. Parking is almost impossible later in the day.

Originally, it was celebrated in a somewhat violent way, but in 1906, the idea of creating an organized *carnival* arose, the proceeds of which would benefit those most in need. Even today, there is an entrance fee, and the proceeds go to charitable institutions.

Festivities start at 3 p.m., and there's always a queue for the tickets to enter the segregated roads. At 2 euros for an adult ticket, it's a low cost for a lot of fun. Celebrations kick off when enormous floats featuring hundreds of hours of professional artistry make their way down the main street, pulled by tractors. It takes over an hour for them to pass, and they go around the circuit twice.

***

Where Mary takes the focus for Easter

March/April: Loulé celebrates the feast of Nossa Senhora da Piedade, the city's patron saint known as the Sovereign Mother, attracts crowds of visitors. This feast has been celebrated for almost five centuries and takes place at two different times: on Easter Sunday (*Festa Pequena*) and fifteen days later (*Festa Grande*). This is considered the most important religious manifestation of the Marian cult south of Fátima in Central Portugal.

***

⦿ São Brás de Alportel

Where the streets are carpeted with flowers

March/April: The Feast of the Flower Torches, also known as Procession of Resurrection in São Brás de Alportel is a unique celebration that has transformed itself over time. For Easter Sunday the streets are decorated with a kilometer-long flower carpet and the men and boys of the town carry elaborate "torches" made up of flowers to celebrate the resurrection of Christ.

***

⦿ Silves

Algarve's living medieval spectacle

August: In Silves, the event of the year is in August, when the town is transported back to medieval times for 10 days, with feasting, dancing, jousting, and shopping. The area around the Praça Al-Muthamid gardens is transformed into a tented area and includes games and events for families and children to enjoy, including traditional archery (watch out for stray flying arrows).

Each night, a professional drama troupe reenacts a different part of Silves' history. The show covers the period from 1189 during the reign of Sancho I and the first Christian conquest of the city through to 1191 and the Muslim reconquest.

At 6 p.m. every day, the events commence with a procession through the streets, which starts from the Praça Al-Muthamid gardens and winds its way all the way to the top of the town outside the cathedral.

The main event in the castle each evening is performances by medieval dance and circus theater groups. There are belly dancers, a medieval music group, a drumming group, troubadours, and Egyptian dancers, not to mention the traveling actors who wander the streets reenacting slavery, drunkenness, and general medieval life.

The streets are transformed into a series of market stalls, bazaars, and food stalls, selling all manner of crafts and homemade goods. You can even exchange your euros for Xelbs, which were the local currency at the time. With an exchange rate of 1:1, it's a shopper's paradise.

***

⊙ **Tavira**

Tavira's candlelit Easter journey

March/April: Tavira is known for its Procession of Senhor dos Passos, which has been drawing visitors for a long time. The procession demonstrates Christ's journey from the Mount of Olives to his death, and it's been held here since as early as 1789. The route is lit by hundreds of candles, making it quite a sight to witness.

***

A southern feast for the senses

September: In September, Tavira holds one of the biggest festivals in southern Portugal, a celebration of the Mediterranean diet, with music and good food. For the 2022 edition, Portugal's top fado singer, Mariza, gave a free open-air concert for thousands in the center of town.

***

⊙ **Vila Real de San Antonio**

The biggest nativity scene in the country

December: Over Christmas and the New Year, Vila Real de San Antonio is home to Portugal's biggest *presépio*, a vast Christmas creche covering some 240 square meters in a local cultural center. Organizers charge a small entry fee. The nativity depicts rural life, sometimes with strong echoes of the eastern Algarve, with models of traditional houses, people, house carts, water mills, beach huts, and salt pans.

***

Celebrate the 1700s

May: In 2023, Vila Real de San Antonio held the inaugural, "Vila Real de Santo António Setecentista," with street parades, banquets, and music meant to celebrate the century of the town's founding in the 1700s. It's so far been repeated each year since.

***

The Islands

The Azores and Madeira's Easter duel

March/April: In both the Azores and Madeira a special tradition is shared: an Easter game called *balamento*. This informal game will begin to be played 8 to 10 days before Easter by both children and adults. Two people agree to play with one another for the period of Lent. The goal is to be the first to say *"balamento"* to the other each day until Easter. The person who has done so the most times, wins. In the end, the loser gives the winner a prize previously agreed on. Today, the prize is almost always a package of Easter almonds, but traditionally, it would usually be sugar cubes or dried figs.

***

⊙ **Azores**

Island-style carnival

February: The islands of the Azores are home to one of the most peculiar forms of *carnival* in Portugal, with balls, dances, theater performances, and water fights.

In Ponta Delgada (the capital of the Azores), the streets welcome a colorful parade of children in costumes, representing their respective school districts. A grand parade stretches late into the night, ending in a spectacular fireworks display.

***

The Azore's Easter pilgrimage

March/April: On the largest island in the Azores archipelago, São Miguel, the Procession of Senhor da Pedra is held on Easter Monday, when locals gather to walk to a chapel on top of a hill to worship an image of Christ.

On the islands of the Azores, roasted young goat is also typical for Easter, along with *folar de linguiça* (a type of sausage). When it comes to sweets, *folar* from Ilha das Flores and *massa sovada* (a treat that's kind of a mix of a rich bread and a cake, often eaten year-round) are all-time favorites.

***

⚲ Madeira

The loudest prelude to carnival

February: Funchal, the island's capital, wakes up on the Friday before Ash Wednesday to the sound of brass bands and *carnival* parades downtown.

The main *carnival* street parade takes place on Saturday evening, with thousands of samba dancers filling the streets.

In Funchal, there are two big *carnival* parades: the Allegorical Parade (*Cortejo Alegórico*), with dozens of groups, and the Clumsy Parade (*Cortejo Trapalhão*), open to everyone.

***

What Easter tastes like in Madeira

March/April: Easter traditions on the islands of Madeira and Porto Santo include chicken stew and goat stew as main dishes. The most traditional sweet is probably a confection called *torrão de açúcar* (literally, sugar lump) which comes in several flavors, with the fruit flavor being the most popular.

National Bests

Carnival: Masks, music, and mayhem

February: In the Portuguese calendar, *carnival* stands as arguably the most significant festival of the year, celebrated across the country with equal enthusiasm. In some places, the holiday is steeped in traditions whose origins are lost in time, while in others, it's more influenced by recent trends.

Some towns have highly organized festivities that go on for five or six days, while others are content with a modest parade involving only children from the local schools.

Carnival embodies a spirit of unrestrained celebration, including pranks that can sometimes go overboard.

While it's no longer a national holiday, most government employees are given the Tuesday off, and schools close for both the Monday and Tuesday, meaning most businesses also take the days off for this optional holiday. Restaurants, cafés, and shops often stay open.

Called *entrudo* in the past, this holiday was taken by the Portuguese to the then-colony of Brazil—not just the concept of a rowdy pre-Lenten celebration but also some of its core elements, like the *Zé Pereiras* and the *Gigantones.*

These are, respectively, a lively musical procession and oversized human-like figures with exaggerated features, both of which can still be found in Portugal and in Brazil.

Later, especially in the second half of the 20th century, Portugal actually imported many aspects of Brazilian *carnival,* which is now the most famous in the world. Elements like colorful (and often sparse) costumes and *samba* (a musical genre strongly associated with *carnival*) have been thriving in Portuguese *carnival* celebrations, particularly in urban areas.

In today's *carnival* celebrations, mask-wearing is a crucial element of the festivities. Although in most cases the mask is a mere accessory, in some other cases, it's one of the most (if not the most) important aspects.

Every year, *carnival* features a theme, and it's usually political. One year, for instance, the then-leaders of the ruling coalition, Pedro Passos Coelho and Paulo Portas, sat together on top of a large military tank while their defense minister, Aguiar Branco, attempted to protect the nation with a single slingshot. This was a direct reference to the strict defense spending cuts in Portugal at the time. When you buy your entrance ticket, make sure you also pick up the free brochure that explains (both in Portuguese and in English) the political nuance of each float.

Not all the floats are political, though… you might see the garden of Eden, celebrities, mythological characters, and much more. Kids and adults alike tend to dress up for the celebrations. During the early days of *carnival,* oranges were thrown at passersby. Revelers, their identities hidden by their costumes, also threw rotten eggs, corn, and other products. Masks had to be prohibited at one point to stop the shenanigans

The traditions surrounding these celebrations also often involve the display and parading of some type of "doll," in many cases representing *Entrudo* itself, involved in a funeral parody, and finally, its destruction: the symbolic death of winter, making way for Lent (and spring).

During *carnival,* it's tradition to eat *filhós de laranja,* which are a kind of doughnut made with flour, sugar, orange, and vanilla.

The general atmosphere is of unrestrained celebration with a generous number of satirical elements of accusation and provocation mixed in, often reflecting recent events. These are delivered mostly with humor, but at times with an offensive tone. No one is spared, and politicians are a favorite target. Until the early-mid 1990s, it was not uncommon for *carnival* celebrations to be a bit more "turbulent" than they are now...

***

Easter: Bread, blessings, and burning Judas

March/April: Easter in Portugal is full of meaningful cultural and gastronomic traditions that began centuries ago. Here, Easter involves religious and cultural traditions often adapted to local traditions and usually include candlelit processions, prayer, vigil, and hymns. The religious celebrations, which start with Lent and Ash Wednesday (right after *carnival*), continue Palm Sunday when many church entrances are decked with palm branches to commemorate Christ's entry into Jerusalem. Holy Thursday and Good Friday are synonymous with reenactments of biblical events and nighttime processions.

Good Friday is a civil holiday and, by then, schools are on spring break. The three-day weekend, paired with longer and sunnier days, makes this a perfect occasion for families to enjoy a short vacation.

Schools take a two-week break, the last until the end of the school year, around mid/late June. Some families opt for taking the whole first week off (Holy Week, often referred to as Easter Week). Good Friday is a public holiday in Portugal, so most have at least a three-day weekend.

On Good Friday you can expect public services to be closed, along with some small shops. Even though this day is a public holiday, the fact that so many people will be traveling or just spending time with friends and family (especially if the weather is nice) means more business opportunities. For that reason, you can expect to find supermarkets, restaurants, and shops open.

Easter Monday is not a holiday in Portugal, but for some people (particularly in villages and in the north), this time is strongly associated with Easter traditions. This, together with the long weekend, means that quite often the small shops that are open on Good Friday will be closed on Easter Monday.

Easter in Portugal is a meaningful time not only for families, but for communities in general… it's not just about religious celebrations but also about sharing food and exchanging gifts in the spirit of peace, joy, and friendship.

Portuguese kids await Easter with anticipation—not really because of the religious celebrations and not (only) because of the school break, but mostly because they'll be receiving gifts. It's a tradition in Portugal for children to receive chocolate eggs or almonds, but also other gifts, like toys, books, or even money. They receive these gifts mostly from their godparents, but quite often also from their grandparents. For many, it's a sort of "small Christmas."

Folar is a kind of sweet bread (can also be savory) that can be exchanged as a gift between godchildren and godparents on Easter Sunday. Sporting a more or less round shape, *folar* can also have two boiled eggs (shell included) in its middle, with two strips of dough making a cross shape over the eggs.

Pão de ló is a beloved sponge cake enjoyed throughout the year in Portugal, but especially so during Easter. Some are still baked in wood-fired ovens and others have a creamy, oozy consistency, while others sport a generous sugar glazing. Each one of them became a symbol of local pride, tradition, and culinary heritage.

For many Portuguese, *pão de ló* has a strong connection with childhood memories. Not only because it was a classic at family gatherings but also because it was the cake so many first got to make as children, gladly (un)helping our mothers or grandmothers.

(Trivia tidbit: Portuguese explorers took *pão de ló* to Japan in the 16th century, where it evolved until it became the cake known today as *kasutera*.)

During Easter celebrations, it's traditional to garnish *pão de ló* with sweet egg threads (*fios de ovos*, in Portuguese) and miniature chocolate eggs to create a little "nest" in the middle of the cake.

Deep cleaning the house on Easter is a common practice in several parts of the country. This serves not only as a spring cleaning of sorts, but also as preparation to receive the *Compasso*. This is when the local priest, followed by a small group of people, enters houses (symbolizing Jesus Christ entering people's homes) carrying the cross to bless the house and the people who live there. Usually, after a short prayer, there is a bit of a chat and some light eating and drinking before the next house is visited. It's common at this time for people to make a money donation to the local church.

One of the oldest Easter traditions is Queima do Judas (Burning of the Judas), where a straw dummy representing Judas Iscariot is burned in a public square as a symbolic act of punishment.

This holiday is celebrated across the country, of course, but many towns have Easter claims to fame of their own, and we've pointed out in this section every notable destination-based Easter event.

But there are also a few ways in which Easter is venerated from region to region, for example:

❖ In the north, one of the most popular traditions is the Procession of Senhor dos Passos, which attracts thousands of people every year. *Senhor dos Passos* literally means "Lord of the Steps" and refers to the image of Christ carrying the cross.

When it comes to Easter eats, here they take pride in its savory varieties of *folar* and its *bolas*, a type of rich bread dough (often including milk and eggs) that has smoked meats like ham, salami, and sausage mixed in. In some cases, the meats will be cut up into pieces and scattered in the dough, in other cases, they will be divided into one or two layers.

Lamb and young goat are popular options in terms of main dishes, generally served roasted with a side of roasted potatoes and other vegetables.

❖ In central Portugal, centuries-old traditions are the key to the celebration. One such tradition, which visitors can witness in some villages, is a dramatic representation of the Passion of Christ that takes place with crosses being carried by hooded men (the hoods being a symbol of mourning). In this part of the country, Easter processions often include streets decorated with flower carpets, especially the Procession of the Burial of the Lord. Usually, these are stunningly elaborate works that last only for a few hours. They are kind of like a mandala, but with flowers.

Here the favorite Easter dishes are often cod and roasted suckling pig. In contrast to the north, this region prefers sweet *folar* for Easter.

❖ In the south, most people will take the opportunity to whitewash their house.

In Alentejo, lamb is a mandatory presence at the Easter table, with *folar* and *queijadas* (a small pastry made with cottage cheese or milk) also appearing on most tables.

In Elvas (Alentejo), *folar* is often shaped like lambs, chicks, and lizards and is then decorated with white almonds and boiled eggs.

In Portalegre, Marvão, and Castelo de Vide, it's common to make a sweet folar in the shape of a lizard: the eyes are made with black-eyed peas, almonds are placed along the body, and a colorful ribbon on the neck.

***

Get your chestnuts roasted

November: In November, many villages and communities celebrate *Magusto*, especially around Nov. 11, St Martin's Day. This is the time for savoring roasted chestnuts and drinking the traditional *jeropiga* and *água-pé*.

5. Beaches

With more than 1,000 miles of coastline and beaches, many of them award winning for cleanliness, accessibility, and environmental awareness, Portugal truly is a beach-lover's paradise.

While the country boasts beaches from the north to the southern coast, the Algarve is by far the most famous beach destination.

Most folks don't travel much further west than Lagos when they visit the Algarve, which is a shame… Some of the most spectacular beaches and prettiest towns are nestled along the furthest southwest and western Algarve coastlines.

Sun's Out, Buns Out—Portugal's Nudist-Friendly Shores

Portugal has surprisingly few official nudist beaches. However, the country has a relaxed attitude towards nudism, and it's acceptable to go without clothes on plenty of beaches.

In fact, over 50 beaches are welcoming to nudists even if they do not have an official nudist friendly status. And this is a country that stays pretty warm even in winter, with temperatures rarely getting below the 50s.

Central Portugal

⦿ Albufeira do Alqueva

Fake lake, real fun

Head to the Albufeira do Alqueva for inland water adventures in Central Portugal. Spanning about 97 square miles, making it the largest artificial lake in Europe, it is a crucial water reservoir and a hub for recreational activities, with calm waters that offer an ideal setting for sailing, kayaking, and paddleboarding (SUP).

A gem for nature enthusiasts, tranquility seekers, and adventure junkies alike, the charm of the lake is complimented by the villages that dot its shores, giving a glimpse into local cultures and traditions.

Fishermen will find excellent opportunities to cast a line, while bird-watchers will marvel at the diversity that thrives here. The unique ecosystem is a haven for many species, making it a prime spot for wildlife observation.

*****

SUP?

Stand-up paddleboarding (SUP) is one of the fastest growing sports in the Algarve, and it's not hard to see why. Conditions here are perfect, even for beginners, to enjoy this sport. Plus, SUP, as well as kayak or canoe, are excellent ways of reaching the Algarve's hidden beaches, caves, and grottos that are un-reachable to the average sunbather.

⊙ Caldas da Rainha

Goldilocks of surf beaches

Foz do Arelho is one of the most famous beaches in the country and a well-loved spot among both surfers and families.

*****

⊙ Setúbal

City to sea in 60 minutes or less

Setúbal is well known for its beaches, which stretch westward from the city. Figueirinha, Coelhos, Galapinhos, and Portinho da Arrábida are all situated one after the other and are within 30 minutes of Setúbal and an hour from Lisbon. They are all wide, sandy, and well-appointed with amenities, making this area one of the best beach escapes in this region.

*****

The Silver Coast's best cliff-and-beach combo

About 20 minutes north of Nazaré, the country's most famous surfing beach, are São Pedro de Moel and Vieira de Leiria (located next to one another), which are two of the most popular beaches in the Silver Coast area, with sandy beaches, dramatic cliffs, and a relaxed atmosphere. Usually you have to choose between cliffs with rocky and/or narrow beaches and sandy beaches without much scenery behind them. Not so here. Vieira de Leiria is also a traditional fishing village, where you'll see boats leave in the morning and come back with fresh catches.

Southern Portugal

The Blue Flag: Portugal's Cleanest, Safest, Most Beautiful Beaches

The Algarve region is home to a number of Blue Flag beaches, and has a reputation for having some of the best beaches in the world.

The iconic Blue Flag is one of the world's most recognized awards for beaches, marinas, and sustainable tourism boats. To be eligible, a beach must meet strict environmental, educational, safety, and accessibility criteria.

Portugal has the 6th highest number of Blue Flag awards, with a total of 440: 398 beaches, 19 marinas, and 23 boats.

All that in mind, it's not surprising the Algarve is home to some of Portugal's best beaches, including nudist beaches...

⚲ Albufeira

Best beach for celebrity spotting

Evaristo Beach near Albufeira has a lovely restaurant overlooking the beach and is the perfect location for exploring and searching the many rock pools. Disabled access is good, with a boardwalk running down to and along the beach. It has excellent facilities and even the chance of some celebrity-spotting too. The restaurant of the same name is right on the beach, with an enviable menu of fish and seafood. It attracts famous and wealthy people, although you can always just order a drink and sit here watching the sunset.

*****

Accessible Algarve: Beaches for everyone

The Algarve Tourist Board website lists 47 accessible beaches in the region, each clickable with details on the beach, the location, how to get there, parking, its amenities, activities available, and lots more information. They even includes a series of accessible itineraries for the regions of Faro, Tavira, Vilamoura, Portimão, and Lagos.

In general, you can expect: "On beaches flying the 'Accessible Beach' flag, people with limited mobility will find access ramps, walkways, handrails, disabled toilets, reserved parking spaces, and restaurant tables that are unobstructed and appropriately sized. Most of the accessible beaches also have an amphibious wheelchair."

Many beaches also have wooden boardwalks, even if they aren't official accessible beaches.

*****

⦿ **Benagil**

Best beach to experience from a boat

East of Carvoeiro is the little fishing village of Benagil. This is still a working fishing village with boats pulled up on the beach at the bottom of the slipway. The beach is unspoiled, although parking is difficult as there is no parking lot, just on-road parking. The limestone cliffs here are stunning, and colorful carved arches form an amazing backdrop to this beach. One of the most iconic and photographed structures must be the Algar de Benagil nearby, which is a cathedral-like cave with arched entrances and a small beach inside. Many people travel by boat to set foot inside this cavernous structure, but beware the tide as you get out of the boat, as you can easily be tipped into the water.

*****

📍 Carvoeiro

The quintessential Algarvian beach

Praia Da Marinha has the views that are so iconic to the Algarve: crumbling cliffs, hidden coves, and incredible arches of rock reaching out into the sea. Marinha is one of several beaches east of Carvoeiro, near Armação de Pêra. Access to the beach is via some steep steps, or you can enjoy the views from the cliff-top walks above. Marinha is a large cove with lots of caves and rock pools to explore. It's a relatively small beach with a lack of tourist facilities or cafés. The color of the sea and sky against the majestic limestone cliffs set it apart and ensure that it is a well-photographed and much-loved beach.

✳✳✳

Stroll above the dunes, spot flamingos below

About 30 minutes east of Carvoeiro is Praia dos Salgados. It's part of one long expanse of beach that stretches for miles, but there are named sections along the way, even if no one quite knows where one ends and the next begins.

Unlike the coast further east, which is backed by cliffs and rocks, Praia dos Salgados has low sand dunes. These are covered over by wooden boardwalks to protect the local environment and nature, and the walkways are ideal for a leisurely and easy stroll.

Beyond the sand dunes lies the Salgados Lagoon. Many migrating birds use the wetlands as a stopover and nest among the reeds. If you're lucky, you can also spot herons and flamingos here, and if you lean over the bridge on the walkway, you can watch the turtles swimming in the water.

✳✳✳

📍 Faro

Flaunt your form in Faro

Praia de Faro is the beach of the Algarve's capital city, Faro. The beach spans several miles and tucked away at the far end, away from the tourists, is the nudist beach.

✳✳✳

⊙ **Ferragudo**

Biggest beach with all the amenities

Situated on the eastern shores of the mouth of the River Arade, at Ferragudo and just across the water from Praia da Rocha and Portimão, is the wide sandy stretch of Praia Grande. It translates as "big beach" and is over half a kilometer long. It has soft sand and a protected bay. The beachside cafés and boats moored in the harbor in the summer months give this a real holiday tourist feel.

There's a wooden walkway that covers about half of the length of the beach, which allows easy access for families or people with reduced mobility. It is the perfect beach to stroll along at sunset or in the early morning in the winter months. At low tide, you can walk through the rock pools all the way round to Praia de Molhe beach.

Most vacationers only walk from the end of the wooden boardwalk to the nearest sun lounger though, so if you're willing to walk a little way further, you can find yourself an unoccupied stretch of beach.

Praia Grande is a popular spot—it's the tourist beach—and can become quite busy in the summer. But it's a great beach for families, with water sports, a lifeguard, and a relatively safe bay for swimming. The northern end of the beach has the imposing feature of the 16th century fort of São João do Arade. Originally built to defend the coast from pirates, the fort is now privately owned and has been lovingly restored.

***

The local's beach

Ferragudo's smaller main beach, Praia da Angrinha, is less developed and looks more like a river beach, complete with a series of old fishing huts scattered behind the main path. There's a large free parking lot here.

You often see the fishermen fixing their nets here, all under the watchful eye of the Coastguard's office and launch. It's a lovely spot to walk along and watch the waves as they skid along the sand.

Praia da Angrinha is the locals' beach—a wide beach backed by the unmistakable gold and red cliffs of the local area. The sea is a mix of estuary and ocean, but the man-made breakwaters for the lighthouses nearby protect the bay and make it safe for swimming. There's a parking area, toilets, an outdoor shower, and a small play park for children. In the summer, you can rent lawn chairs and umbrellas, and there's a full lifeguard service. A mark-out volleyball court appears and competitions take place.

***

⊚ Monte Clérigo

Wild, windswept, and wonderfully quiet

On Algarve's west coast, this delightful beach with wide-open sand, decent body-boarding waves, and the most stunning small black rocks that wash up on the beach…

The Algarve's west coast has an unspoiled feel, with wide, sandy beaches bracing themselves against the full force of the Atlantic Ocean. This beach is in the Vicentina Coast Natural Park, which is an area of outstanding natural beauty. It has a couple of cafés, a restaurant, toilets, and lifeguards in the summer. But it is in winter when this beach comes to life, with Atlantic swells and bracing fresh air. It's the perfect place to wrap up and go for a walk along the sand.

***

⊚ Olhão

Catch the ferry, dodge the crowds

Your average tourist doesn't come to Olhão because they say there is no beach. They don't know that just a short ferry ride away and a stroll across the dunes there are two of the best beaches in Europe, on Armona and Culatra Islands, both car-free and worth a visit in themselves. These offer a chance get completely away from the crowds. The beaches on this little island are pristine, white-sand stretches with very few visitors at any time of year.

***

⊚ Portimão

A treasure only revealed at low tide

Praia Dos Três Irmãos is the eastern end of Alvor beach, named after the three jutting rocks or "Três Irmãos" (three brothers) that extend into the sea, creating a stunning backdrop and a beautiful beach location to relax and enjoy. At low tide, you can walk along the adjoining sandy bays that each have their own rock arches, caves, and limestone cliffs to enjoy. There are plenty of facilities on the beach, including toilets, disabled access, excellent restaurants, and a summer lifeguard service.

***

⊙ Praia da Luz

Perfect for pint-sized paddlers

Praia da Luz, with its wide sandy outlook, is perfect for walking, sunbathing or building sandcastles, complete with new wooden boardwalks to increase accessibility, great for families. The sea is calm and shallow, and gets deeper slowly with a gentle pitch, which makes this beach perfect for those with small children. The beach can be busy in the height of summer, but a short walk along the beach towards the Rocha Negra, and you can have the beach pretty much to yourself.

***

⊙ Tavira

Topless in Tavira

Praia do Homem Nu is one of the official nude beaches of the Algarve. The name translates as "Beach of the Naked Man," in case there was any confusion about what to expect. The beach is located in Tavira, and it's an easy trip from the nearby tourist villages. A Blue Flag beach, with white sands and clean, bracing waters.

***

Strut your stuff at a sandy cemetery

Praia do Barril is located on the Ilha de Tavira, just west of the town of Tavira. This beach has a huge stretch of white sand, and you're almost guaranteed some peace and quiet here. The western end of the beach is an official nudist beach.

The beach is most famous for its Anchor Graveyard or "Cemitério das Âncoras" hidden amongst the dunes. The sight of hundreds of rusting and rotting anchors all lined up in rows is quite something. The area used to be a major tuna fishing area, and the anchors were used to tie the tuna nets in place. With the decline of the industry, they left the anchors to rot, and they are still there to this day.

***

⦿ Vila do Bispo

A beach for any activity

Near Vila do Bispo in western Algarve, Cordoama is a soft, sandy beach that joins Castelejo beach at low tide. The border between these two beaches forms a series of rock formations and is a favored spot for sea anglers. The beach is over a mile long, with plenty of space for everyone. It's a favorite surf spot, as well as great for dog-walking in the winter and a famous spot for paragliding.

***

⦿ Vila Real de Santo António

The warmest waters off Portugal

The beach at Vila Real de Santo António is quieter than Algarve's other beaches typically are, and the sea is just a little warmer than it is further to the west in the Algarve. The average sea temperature in summer is 70°F and 68.4°F in autumn.

6. Adventures

Portugal is a fantastic place for seeking adventures in the outdoors. Whether hiking the trails that crisscross the country, exploring the countryside with your dog, biking the oceanfront routes up and down the coast, bird watching in the natural parks, or playing on the water, just about anything you want to do in nature is available here.

Plus, with mild weather year-round, there's no bad time of year to be outdoorsy.

Northern Portugal

⊙ Braga

Portugal's last great wilderness

About an hour from Braga lies Peneda-Gerês National Park, at the most northern tip of the country, known for its natural beauty and various ecosystems. Hike rugged mountains, explore dense forests, and enjoy pristine rivers and waterfalls. Gerês is also home to diverse wildlife, including the Garrano horses and the Iberian wolf.

For outdoor enthusiasts, the park offers a range of activities, like mountain biking and canoeing. Hiking trails wind through it, leading to viewpoints where you can take in panoramic vistas of the surrounding landscape. The park is also home to traditional villages where visitors can experience local culture and cuisine.

***

⊙ Douro Valley

Biking through wine country

Some of the best locations to cycle are in the Douro Valley, as many of its roads are flat and paved, and you can cycle through the verdant, lush landscape surrounded by vineyards and open countryside.

***

⊙ **Porto**

The palace Porto refused to forget

The Palácio Cristal Gardens is a lovely outdoor space in Porto that includes a restaurant and a terrace overlooking the lake on the grounds. Before you settle down for a coffee or a snack, tour the "aromatic plants" garden, the medicinal garden, the rose garden, the "feelings garden," and more themed beds. The landscaping is a view unto itself, but the grounds are also laid out to offer views of the Douro River. Various cultural and social events, shows, and other entertainments are held here… come for concerts, circuses, exhibitions, and sporting events as well as the venue itself.

The misleadingly named Palácio Cristal is actually a concrete arena that looks more like an alien spacecraft than a building. The structure that stood on the site before was, in fact, a crystal palace designed by a British architect and styled after London's version. It played host to a number of expositions and was home to one of the largest pipe organs in the world. It was demolished in 1951 to much dissent (it is noted that the organ was destroyed by hammer), so in protest people continued to call it the crystal palace.

***

Portugal's most bike-friendly city

The best city for biking in Portugal is Porto, with a growing network of around 30 miles of bike lanes. The city has been investing in cycling infrastructure, making it easier to explore both the historic center and the scenic riverfront by bike.

Porto's compact size, combined with its mix of flat riverside routes and more challenging hills, offers options for casual cyclists and seasoned riders alike. One of the most popular rides is along the Douro River, from the city center all the way out to the Atlantic coast at Foz do Douro—flat, beautiful, and dotted with cafés and photo opps.

Many hotels and shops now offer bike rentals and e-bikes, and some of the best views of the city are best reached on two wheels. Plus, the newer riverside developments and boardwalks make for breezy, low-stress rides ideal for families or travelers just looking for a relaxed day out.

***

The classiest booze cruise

The Douro River feeds into the Atlantic at Porto, after crossing the country from Spain, and it's one of the most popular cruising routes in or around Portugal. From a half day to over a week, you can opt for any kind of itinerary that suits your schedule, some of the longer cruises even cross the border and include stops in Spain. Glide through a UNESCO World Heritage landscape, passing through steep terraced vineyards, ancient villages, and dramatic gorges—many of which are hard to access otherwise.

As well as being the best way to see the stunning natural beauty of northern Portugal, the river is also the home to Portugal's world-renowned wine culture. A Douro wine cruise is one of the most unique and rewarding ways to experience this region. The Douro Valley is the birthplace of Port wine, one of the world's most iconic fortified wines, but it also produces high-quality red and whites. Many cruises include exclusive access to wine estates (*quintas*) for tastings and tours.

The major cruise lines start and/or end in Porto or Vila Nova de Gaia. Smaller boutique lines, though, may also leave from Barca d'Alva, Réguam, or Pinhão, especially if they are wine focused.

Plus, these cruises are on smaller boats, meaning you get a more intimate experience.

***

Steam With A Scene

Queer saunas are a staple of Portugal's LGBTQ+ nightlife, offering a welcoming space to unwind, connect, and enjoy some steamy socializing. These saunas aren't just about relaxation—they're a part of the local queer culture, especially in cities like Lisbon and Porto.

Whether you're visiting solo or with friends, these saunas are a great way to meet locals, take a break from the bars, and experience a side of queer life that's refreshingly open and unapologetically social.

Porto's hotspots (literally)

In Porto, two of the most popular gay saunas are Sauna Thermas 205 and Sauna Camões. Both spots offer modern facilities with steam rooms, dry saunas, private cabins, dark rooms, and bar areas. Thermas 205 is known for its relaxed vibe and mixed-age crowd, while Camões tends to attract a younger, more party-ready crowd and often hosts themed nights or events.

Central Portugal

⦾ Almada

Where Lisbon's dogs go to unleash

Parque da Paz, located just across the river from Lisbon in Almada, is one of the most beloved destinations for the four-legged residents of the area—and their humans too. With wide open lawns, shaded walking paths, and dedicated dog-friendly zones, it's the perfect spot for a game of fetch or a leisurely stroll. Locals love it for its peaceful atmosphere, scenic lake, and occasional dog meetups, especially on weekends. Whether your pup wants to run wild or just sniff around, Parque da Paz is a little slice of doggy heaven.

***

⦾ Caldas da Rainha

See the 5th wonder

About an hour inland from Nazaré, you'll find the Mira d'Aire Caves, a mesmerizing network of limestone caves and one of the country's most impressive natural wonders. Explore the underground chambers adorned with stunning stalactites and stalagmites, walk along illuminated paths, and marvel at the geological formations that took millions of years to form. Guided tours provide fascinating insights into the caves' history and geological significance.

***

From royal grounds to urban oasis

Dom Carlos I Park is Caldas da Rainha's best-known park and a true icon. Originally built by King Dom João V to support the nearby thermal hospital, the park underwent significant changes at the end of the 19th century, transforming it into a leisure area that is still cherished by the locals. If you go there on a sunny weekend, expect to find it crowded: some kids will be playing soccer, others will be in the children's playground, and others will be simply exploring the green areas of the park.

Like most parks created around that time in Europe, it features a lake with a small island in the middle, a bandstand, and boulevards lined with trees and adorned with statues. Near the lake, you can't miss the so-called pavilions, designed at the end of the 19th century, and meant to serve the thermal hospital. However, they never fulfilled their intended use, and over the years were repurposed to house military barracks, a police station, and a high school, having been abandoned in the early 2000s.

Today, the inside of these pavilions is severely damaged but the facades still retain much of their original beauty and are one of the main aesthetic elements of Caldas da Rainha.

***

Lagoon leisure

When it comes to water adventures, it's not all open seas... You can also explore inshore waters, like the Óbidos reservoir lagoon—the largest coastal lagoon system in the country. Take kayak or stand up paddleboard (SUP) tours, private or group boat tours through the lagoon, see its islands, and even hike through the banks and crannies of the reservoir.

***

Historically healing waters

Caldas de Monchique, about 3 miles from Monchique town, is a relaxing and attractive village. It's said to be a former favorite locale of the Portuguese nobility for its healing waters. Today, it's a quiet health resort with hotels and therapy treatments for relaxation, and restaurants, cafés, handicraft shops, and lovely squares for entertainment.

⊙ **Cascais**

Waves, wind, and world-class races

Cascais Bay is among the best regatta locations in the world and regularly hosts sailing's most prestigious events. Its unique geography—sheltered enough for spectators, yet exposed to strong Atlantic winds—makes it ideal for competitive sailing. The bay has become a regular stop on the international circuit, drawing elite sailors and sleek vessels from across the globe.

Many international races take place in Portuguese waters, including the Tall Ships Race, which brings a fleet of towering masts and maritime tradition to the coastline, and the Volvo Ocean Race, one of the most grueling endurance sailing events in the world, which has made multiple stopovers in Lisbon. April to October is the prime season, with most international races and local regattas scheduled during this window.

Whether you're a sailing enthusiast or just enjoy the spectacle, regatta season turns the coast into a lively blend of sport, celebration, and sea spray—complete with festival energy, harborside parties, and unbeatable Atlantic sunsets.

***

⊙ **Coimbra**

An Enlightenment-era Eden

Coimbra's Jardim Botânico (Botanical Garden) is the largest of its kind in Portugal—you'll need more than a single visit to see all it has to offer. However, if you can spare a few minutes, allow yourself to at least take a look around, have a seat, and enjoy the much-needed shade, especially in the summer months.

This garden, founded in 1772 by the Marquis of Pombal, is divided into different areas representing different latitudes and climates, filled with trees and plants from various locations around the world, with a total of over 1,200 different types of plants. The Neo-Classical fountain and the double staircase feature high among the points of interest in this garden.

***

Best park for kids

Parque Verde and Parque da Cidade Manuel Braga in Coimbra are excellent green area if you have kids. Here, they can run free and stretch their legs or just lay down on the grass near the river. There's also a small playground, which is right in front of a series of cafés, restaurants, and, not surprisingly, an ice cream shop. It's also a destination for dog owners.

***

A park for romantics

Jardim da Sereia, or, Mermaid Garden, is a scenic garden with strong Baroque influences, designed after French and Italian gardens of the 18th century. It's famous for its luxuriant vegetation and the statues scattered throughout the park, but the real showpiece of the garden is undoubtedly the Fonte das Lágrimas, or Fountain of Tears. This gorgeous ornate fountain was inspired by Portugal's famous tragic love story of Inês de Castro and King Pedro I. Legend goes that the tears shed by Inês after being murdered turned into little springs that feed this charming fountain.

***

The Legend of Inês de Castro and King Pedro I

Every Portuguese person knows the macabre story of Inês de Castro and King Pedro I, sometimes called the Romeo and Juliet of Portugal—though their story is arguably even more dramatic and haunting. Their forbidden love defied politics and royal expectations, ultimately ending in tragedy.

Inês, a lady-in-waiting of noble Galician descent, fell in love with Pedro, the heir to the Portuguese throne, during his marriage to another woman. After his wife's death, Pedro sought to make Inês his queen, but their union was strongly opposed by his father, King Afonso IV, who feared her family's influence over the Portuguese court.

Despite the opposition, Pedro and Inês continued their relationship and even had children together. But in 1355, while Pedro was away, King Afonso ordered Inês's execution. She was brutally murdered in front of her children at the Monastery of Santa Clara-a-Velha in Coimbra.

Overcome with grief and rage, Pedro led a rebellion against his father. After ascending the throne in 1357, he exacted revenge on Inês's killers—reportedly having their hearts ripped out while still alive. But his most enduring act of devotion came after her death: Pedro claimed that he and Inês had been secretly married, and in a twisted display of love and power, he had her body exhumed, dressed in royal robes, and seated beside him on the throne. Courtiers were forced to kneel before her skeletal remains and kiss her decaying hand in homage.

To this day, the tombs of Pedro and Inês lie facing each other in the Monastery of Alcobaça, so that, as legend holds, they may gaze upon one another and reunite in the afterlife.

***

Views and verses

Penedo da Saudade, or, "Rock of Longing," is a park and viewpoint, built in 1849, with incredible panoramic views of the Mondego River and the Coimbra skyline. The gardens are laid out on terraces that look out over the city, with benches, walking paths, and lots of flora to enjoy in any season.

It's closely linked to the university, and its unique rock walls and formations are adorned with dozens of plaques commemorating events linked to academic life and poems by students.

According to local folklore, after the murder of his beloved Inês, King Pedro I would retreat here to mourn. The romantic atmosphere of the garden, with its panoramic views and melancholic inscriptions, has inspired poets throughout the years, particularly during the Romantic era. João de Deus penned a poem called *Penedo da Saudade*, a tribute to the "tears of mad longing" that Pedro is said to have shed here.

***

Portugal in miniature

Portugal dos Pequenitos, created with children in mind, features scaled-down replicas of Portuguese monuments and traditional architecture.

One section features traditional architecture from various regions, including manor houses, houses of nobles and seigneurs, along with homes from orchards, gardens, mills, and pillories. Another area displays Portuguese monuments. And a third is dedicated to former Portuguese colonies, as well as monuments from Madeira and the Azores.

***

Flora of a forgotten Portugal

Quinta das Lágrimas, the "Estate of Tears," is renowned for its garden and its association with the tragic love story of Pedro and Inês (see page 147).

Covering about 45 acres, it's home to a 19th-century palace (now a luxury hotel) and fantastic gardens where you'll find exotic species, some of which are over two hundred years old. The southern slope is covered in a forest, ideal for long walks, and the first Medieval Garden in Portugal was recently created in homage to Pedro and Inês. This garden grows 50 species of plants that were specially selected after being confirmed as being present in the region before the Age of Discoveries, making it as authentic to the period as possible.

This estate has been used as the apocryphal setting for the famous love story in many literary and poetic recountings of the legend, and though it's not the real location, the garden is nonetheless themed for them.

A small stream called "Channel of Loves" winds through the gardens, which, according to legend, carried love letters between the estate and the royal palace. After her murder, the waters are said to have run red with her blood… even though there's record of her being killed elsewhere.

***

Where to get away from it all

Craving something with less human interference? Head over to Mata Nacional do Choupal or to the Arzila Swamp Natural Reserve, only 8 miles outside of Coimbra. All along the Mondego, you'll find parks and river beaches, like the one in Palheiros do Zorro, a 15-minute drive from Coimbra.

***

Favorite for Fido

Coimbra's dog park, Parque Canino Municipal, was inaugurated in 2021. Dogs can exercise and socialize over an area of 1,200 square meters, divided into 800 for big dogs and 400 for small dogs. It offers all the amenities you'd want, including water fountains for dogs, bag dispensers, plus equipment like a jumping barrier with three different heights, a board, a climb-up, and a gymkhana with nine posts for big dogs and a jumping hoop, a tunnel, a board, a climb-up, and a gymkhana for small dogs. Fully enclosed and well shaded by trees and a pergola, this is a great destination for dogs and their humans.

***

See it all by foot in Coimbra

This route starts near the river, with the highest point being the University of Coimbra. From there, you'll just be going down towards the river again. Without any stops, this route takes you a bit under two (very easy-going) hours. Think of the uphills as cardio with culture mixed in!

1-Day Route:

1. Largo da Portagem
2. Rua Ferreira Borges
   a. Rua do Arco Almedina and Rua de Quebra Costas
3. Santa Cruz Church
4. Jardim da Manga
5. Sé Velha (Old Cathedral)
6. Machado de Castro National Museum
7. Sé Nova (New Cathedral)
8. University of Coimbra and Joanina Library

9. Jardim Botânico (Botanical Garden)
10. Rua Estrela
    a. Parque Verde and Parque da Cidade Manuel Braga
    b. Café Santa Cruz
    c. Rua de Quebra Costas

Depending on how much time you have, you may need to skip one or two stops. If you look at the map, you may feel tempted to consider doing this route by starting in the parking lot near Parque da Cidade Manuel Braga and doing all the stops in reverse order, but traffic and road works don't make this a pleasant drive. In any case, you'll always have to walk uphill to get to the stops that are higher up in the city, like the university and the Machado de Castro National Museum.

***

⊚ Lisbon

Best hike near Lisbon

Monsanto Forest Park, on Lisbon's city limits, is an area of around 2,470 acres (about 4 square miles) and known as Lisbon's lung. It has playgrounds, picnic areas, trails, sports facilities, and beautiful views of the city and the river's estuary, among other things. Although it's not officially a dog park, they are welcomed in, so it's also a favorite park for dog owners.

***

Lisbon's lush retreat

The iconic Gulbenkian Garden in Lisbon, covering an area of around 22 acres, is one of the most beloved in the city. Many of these gardens will have a playground and at least one small café with seats outside.

***

Authentic tours with local experts

Cooltour Lisbon is a well-regarded tour company that specializes in guided experiences around Lisbon and beyond. Known for its knowledgeable local guides, friendly atmosphere, and insider access, Cooltour is a great choice for experiencing Lisbon through a more authentic, well-curated lens. As well as guided walking or driving tours that cover Lisbon's most iconic sites, they also offer day tours to Sintra, Cascais, Fátima, Évora, and other destinations. These trips often include hotel pickup and skip-the-line access to popular monuments like Pena Palace or the Sanctuary of Fátima. There are also themed tours, such as food and wine, street art and contemporary Lisbon, Jewish heritage, tile tours, and literary routes.

* * *

⦿ Setúbal

Trails and tastings

The Arrábida Natural Park combines limestone cliffs, crystal-clear turquoise waters, and pristine beaches. The park's diverse flora and fauna, combined with its rough landscape, make it a popular spot for hiking, diving, and beach relaxation. The area is also home to vineyards and wineries, where one can sample regional wines and indulge in local gastronomy.

* * *

Portugal's wild island secret

The Berlengas Archipelago, a group of islands about 30 minutes off the coast of Peniche, is a protected nature reserve and a UNESCO Biosphere Reserve—and it is stunning. Its rocky cliffs and secluded coves create a haven for an abundance of birds and marine life to spot, and fishing is regulated but allowed. A ferry takes you to the main island, Berlenga Grande, from which you can explore walking trails, visit the 17th-century fort, or relax on its secluded beaches. Only about 30 people live on the island permanently, and visitors are restricted to 350 people per day.

* * *

⦿ Óbidos

Best birdwatching in the country

Lagoa de Óbidos is the largest coastal lagoon system in Portugal and is well known not only for its beauty but also for its fauna. It's said to be the best place to spot water birds in the country, with 175 species confirmed here. It also provides a key nesting spot for migratory birds, with many stopping to winter here. The park offers hides, lookout towers, and a pedestrian path along the lagoon. You may see any number of species of gulls, ducks, waders, birds of prey, and all kinds of migratory birds.

Look out for flamingo, black-winged stilt, Kentish plover, greater ringed plover, grey plover, whimbrel, Eurasian curlew, red heron, bar-tailed godwit, black-billed sandpiper, common sandpiper, sandpiper, common greenshank, common tern, and great cormorant.

***

⊙ Setúbal

Best chance to see dolphins in the region

For a fun day trip, take a boat from the port of Setúbal to visit the Sado Estuary, a natural reserve where you can see various sea birds. If you're lucky, you might also see the local bottlenose dolphins, one of the smallest and most endangered bottlenose populations in Europe.

***

Urban escape: hiking minutes from the city

Serra da Arrábida, located about 7.5 miles from the Setúbal city center, is an ideal place for hiking and enjoying stunning views and natural surroundings. Towering limestone cliffs plunge into turquoise waters, while dense Mediterranean vegetation — including oak, strawberry trees, and wild herbs — perfumes the air. Trails wind through shaded valleys, past ancient monasteries, and up to panoramic viewpoints overlooking the Atlantic and the Tróia Peninsula. Whether you're after a peaceful forest walk or a challenging coastal hike, Arrábida offers a perfect blend of wilderness and beauty — all just minutes from the city.

***

⊙ Sintra

Head for the hills (with your hound)

The greener areas of the Sintra hills are a favorite escape for dogs and their humans, especially on weekends. Shaded forest paths, cool mountain air, and wide-open trails make it the perfect playground for four-legged adventurers. Whether you're strolling beneath mossy oaks or climbing up to misty viewpoints, you're likely to meet plenty of pawsome friends along the way—tails wagging, tongues out, and ready to explore. Don't forget to pack water and a few treats—for both of you!

***

Donkeys, dirt, and discovery

Get out to the countryside without leaving the city. In the Sintra-Cascais Natural Park you can follow trails through nature, ride bikes, horses, or donkeys, and pick vegetables. This area is called Quinta do Pisão (managed by the municipality of Cascais but in the natural park) and it's a favorite of families and dog owners from both municipalities.

***

Oldest working lighthouse in the region

In Cascais, walk to the Farol da Guia, one of the oldest active lighthouses in Portugal. From there, follow the excellent walking/bike path along the coastline of rugged seaside cliffs into downtown Cascais.

***

Southern Portugal

⊙ **Alcoutim**

Modern-day pilgrimage

The self-guided walking route, the Via Algarviana, is a 300-kilometer (186-mile) walking trail with 14 sections, each with accommodations and refreshment stops at the beginnings and ends. The route is based on a pilgrimage route that took worshippers to the Sagres promontory, where the relics of St. Vincent were allegedly found.

This long-distance trail allows you to discover the Algarve by foot or bike, from Alcoutim to Cabo de São Vicente. And as a bonus, there are 18 short-distance paths, 10 audio-guided routes, and 4 themed routes you can opt to take within the network. The Percurso Pedestre Cultural (the Cultural Walking Trail), for example, reaches from Alcoutim at the Spanish border to the Cape São Vicente in the west. There are also six connecting trails that link the trail to the coast along the Algarve. Although it's a footpath, it's also suitable for mountain biking and horse riding.

The Via Algarviana has an excellent official website, with maps and information highlighting the routes and wildlife you can encounter along the way as it weaves its route through small villages, towns, and the open countryside: https://viaalgarviana.org/en/.

***

⊚ Alentejo

The best way to explore Alentejo

A vineyard region with great roads for biking is the Alentejo, which will also give you the chance to explore small, rural villages, and a traditional farming landscape.

***

⊚ Aveiro

Where pets feel at home

Boasting many gardens and parks, Aveiro is very dog-friendly. If you're planning on relocating with your pet, put the neighborhoods in the Alboi area at the top of your list.

***

⊚ Cacela Velha

Best low-tide beach walk

Walk down a path from the village of Cacela Velha to the water's edge. At low tide, you can wade through the lagoon waters, re-emerge onto land, and then swim in the waters of the Atlantic. This little excursion is a smash hit with visitors.

***

⊚ **Carvoeiro**

Best way to see Benagil

Not far from Carvoeiro is Benagil, which is home to stunning sea caves. The most common way to see them is to take a bouncy boat ride out to this incredible natural landmark. Tour boats leave frequently and from pretty much any nearby town—you can even take a day cruise there from Lisbon.

But if you want to get more up close and personal—and you're feeling strong—take a kayak or stand-up paddle tour there from Benagil beach. If you do, you'll be able to get to the beaches that boat tourists can't.

***

⊚ **Faro**

Birdwatcher's paradise

Famous for being a wildlife haven, Ria Formosa Natural Park in eastern Algarve starts just west of Faro and stretches for about 37 miles, up to Cacela Velha at the eastern end. A mecca for birdwatchers, the Ria Formosa is a complex environment of coastal lagoons with five barrier islands and two peninsulas. It's great for walking, hiking, cycling, kayaking, water sports, and spotting flamingos.

The long string of barrier islands that run parallel to the mainland separate it from the Atlantic, and the result of this topography has a great variety of habitats and exceptional biodiversity. There are saltpans and marshes, canals, lagoons, woods, and farmland, all home to the various flora and fauna that thrive here. More than 300 species of birds, including waders, ducks, and herons, have been sighted in this wetland, and in many places flamingos abound. There's also unique marine life here, including seahorses.

The area surrounding the park still has traditional fishing communities with their own unique cultural heritage. It's an atmospheric stretch of coast, and one of Portugal's most important wetlands.

This is also an excellent place to hike, with its 37 miles of unspoiled coastline. The area has a network of paths and bridges that connect the islands with the mainland, through lagoons teeming with wildlife. And the best part? The routes are traffic free.

***

Trails, tides, and a touch of history

Take a trip to the Quinta do Marim reserve, part of the Ria Formosa Natural Park, just to the east of town. Hiring a bike in Olhão would be a good option. The reserve, a landscape of dunes, salt marshes, and pine woodlands, has waymarked dirt trails and picnic tables. It is a good place for birdwatching. At the water's edge, there is a tidal mill that operated until 1970. It used the tides to turn its millstones and grind cereal.

***

Buffet of boating bliss

Faro is a great starting point for marine tours, including boat trips to the Ilha da Barreta, also known as Desert Island, and to the island of Culatra. You can also sign up for a dolphin-watching tour from here.

***

Experience a 150-million-year-old rock

The Rocha Negra, as the name suggests, is a magnificent section of black rock near Faro in the Algarve. Supposedly created 150 million years ago and formed by hot volcanic lava cascading over the sandstone cliffs, it's an impressive piece of geography. You can hike along the top of the cliffs and enjoy the magnificent, far-reaching views. The route is described as a challenging hiking trail, so wear something suitable on your feet.

***

Birds-eye view of Faro

For the best views of Faro in the Algarve, climb to the top of the cathedral tower, from which you'll not only get a birds-eye view of the town, but also the coast and nearby islands.

***

"Turn left at the salt pile..."

From the entrance of Ludo Park, take the first turn right off the main dirt track that runs along the lagoon, taking you past saltpans and to a mound of salt clearly visible from a distance. Turn left at the salt pile and follow a track leading to a woodland.

Emerging out of the narrow wood you enter a different world. There is a golf course and the suburb of millionaire mansions called Quinta do Lago. From one bird hide, you look out over São Lourenço lake, the golf course, and the mansions beyond.

After the hide, the track will take you back to the lagoon's edge, where there is a second hide for birdwatchers. Follow the lagoon's edge, up to the Ancão footbridge. If you cross over the bridge and walk the few meters, which is the full width of Faro Island, you can take a dip in the Atlantic.

Cross back over the bridge, turn left and after a 15-minute walk, you'll come to an attractive lakeside restaurant called The Shack, a great place to stop for refreshments.

***

⦿ **Ferragudo**

Boating with biologists

One of the best experiences by boat has to be a tour out to cruise alongside a family of dolphins or go whale watching along the Algarve coast. WildWatch Tours in Ferragudo prides themselves on their tours, which are guided by marine biologists, and they are keen to promote ecotourism.

***

Take the scenic route to Silves

Take a boat trip up the River Arade from the fishing village of Ferragudo and approach Silves from the riverfront. Step off the boat and admire one of the town's symbols: the 14th century Roman bridge. It's been classified as a monument of public interest and is now only used by pedestrians. Enjoy the views across town and the ducks paddling in the water. And make sure to spot the nesting white storks that have made Silves their home. You'll see their nests balancing on chimneys and turrets and hear their clattering as they greet each other.

***

⊙ Furnazhinhas

Best springtime hike

A favorite walk in the spring starts and ends in the hill village Furnazhinhas. This village lies at the eastern end of the long-distance walk, Via Algarviana, and not far from the River Guadiana that borders Spain. PR9 and PR10 lead south and north from the village, one to the reservoir at Odeleite and the other follows the elusive course of the Beco da Maria Galega, a narrow undulating stream.

In spring, the hills are awash with rock cistus, blowsy white blooms with a crimson and yellow heart, and tiny white flowers speckle the surface of the stream. The village itself is a delight, and you can walk down to the floor of the reservoir (and back up again) or meander through the valley, following the stream. If you're feeling particularly fit you could do both, but remember to bring a picnic as the small mini-market in the village is often closed and there isn't a restaurant.

***

⊙ Lagoa

Next-level sand art

Sand City is located on the EN125 between the Lagoa and Porches roundabouts and is open from April to October. Recently moved from its original spot near Guia, it has now expanded and is home to 55,000 tons of sand spread out over 6 hectares of outdoor exhibition space. The team of international sculptors has created entertaining sculptures of celebrities, places, characters, and scenes all from reinforced sand.

***

A water park for the whole family

The Slide & Splash water park in Lagoa is open from April to October. Slide & Splash offers water fun for all the family in a vast area of about 10 acres. Located in Estômbar-Lagoa, the park has a huge area with lawns and sun loungers, as well as aquatic attractions and rides for all tastes and ages. The names of some of the rides will give you an idea what to expect: The Corkscrew, Banzai, Black Hole, Plunge, Tornado, Kamikaze, and the newest addition, The Big Wave. They also have various restaurants, a convenience store, massages and a fish spa, and an area for live shows and demonstrations of birds of prey and macaws.

***

⑨ Monchique

The other Algarve route

The Algarve is famed for its cycling routes, but most people stick to hugging the coastline. Cyclists and motorbike enthusiasts in the know, however, also enjoy the more intrepid, winding, scenic routes of the Serra de Monchique. The Serra de Monchique is also popular with hikers and picnickers, with plenty of fountains and springs to drink the famous water from along the trails. It's ideal for birdwatching, scavenging for mushrooms, and seeking inspiration for artists and photographers… but it's also just a great place to retreat and relax.

From Monchique town, you ascend to the two biggest mountains in the Algarve—but they aren't trails for the faint hearted… Fóia reaches 902 meters and Picota 773 meters, both with breathtaking views over the Serra. From Fóia you can enjoy the panoramic views of the west coast, and from Picota, of the west Algarve and the reservoirs.

The route to Fóia is better known and has many roadside restaurants on the journey to the peak, with spectacular views of the countryside and coastline.

***

⑨ Olhão

A ferry to escape the modern world

From Olhão, jump on the ferry to the nearby (car-free) islands of Armona, Culatra, and Farol, where you'll be enchanted by the white-sand beaches, lagoons, great restaurants, bars, shopping and markets. Few people live on these islands permanently, and it's like stepping into another world.

***

⊚ Praia da Luz

Hike there, bus back

From Praia da Luz there are walking trails to Porto de Mós beach (about 2 miles along the cliff path) and towards Sagres (Burgau is about 3 miles away). There are bus links back to Luz from both locations. These are great walks up along the cliffs.

***

Downtime with donkeys

Looking for some affection from animals? The Associação Bamboo is a local animal rescue charity for dogs and donkeys just to the west of Praia da Luz.

***

Aid in the Algarve

If you're looking for a worthwhile place to spend some time, try volunteering at Madrugada Portugal, which offers support to people in the Algarve who are affected by a life-limiting illness. Their Madrugada Centre in Praia da Luz helps people through counseling, therapeutic and creative activities, complementary therapies, advice, and education. They are always looking for volunteers to support their work and help with fundraising. They also have a charity shop in town, staffed by volunteers.

***

⊚ Silves

Unofficial dog run

Although it wasn't created for dogs and is intended for everyone's use, the riverside in Silves has a lovely set of paths and trails that are popular with dog owners, as well as joggers, walkers, bikers, and other outdoor activity seekers.

***

Most scenic saddle experience

The Country Riding Center at Silves is open for riders of all experience levels, including beginners. Professional riders are on hand to teach you how to ride a horse. You can take rides through the hillsides to admire views of the Monchique Mountains and beyond.

***

Iron mine turned theme park

Outside of Silves is the Parque de Mina, a theme park centered around an old iron ore mine. The park highlights the workings of the mine along with a range of activities in the surrounding parkland, which has plenty of picnic spots under the trees. You can also visit their on-site *medronho* distillery and tour the 18th century manor house. For children there is a small petting zoo with a range of animals to feed from dwarf goats to Vietnamese pigs.

***

Dam good walking

The area around Silves is perfect for hiking and walking, with trails mapped out for you. The Barragem do Arade nearby is a favorite spot for walkers, with its 9.5-mile (15-kilometer) circular trail around the dam. The area is teeming with wildlife and birds, great for nature lovers.

***

Where every street leads to a fortress

The turret of one of the main City Gates of Silves, the Torreão da Porta da Cidade, is the only one of the four archways to the *almedina* old town that stands today, and it's an impressive sight, hinting at the fortress-like protection once afforded to the occupants of the city. It's a tall structure, creating images of biblical-sized enemies and soldiers attacking each other.

Today it has the more genteel purpose of housing the municipal library. If you head up to the entrance of the castle, you'll come to the statue of Sancho I of Portugal, known as the Populator, who was the second king of Portugal.

A climb up the narrow and cobbled streets from the arch will lead you to the Cathedral of Silves, which is one of the Algarve's few remaining gothic monuments. Entrance is only 1.50 euro.

But you can get there from nearly anywhere... in Silves, all roads lead up to the castle, the town is full of winding cobbled streets, tucked away tiny shops and cafés, and historical delights.

***

⊙ Tavira

Birdwatching on a budget

The ferry to Tavira Island from Tavira town is the best-value bird-watching trip. For just 2.20 euros, you can board the ferry for the 55-minute round trip on which you'll see flamingos, waders, and a host of other species. About eight minutes in, on the left, you'll often see flamingos feeding, particularly between November and March. At Quatro Águas, one of the stops, terns wheel and dive for fish.

***

Bike there, train back

Leave Tavira on your bike following the signs for Santa Luzia—there is a bicycle lane for the short distance to this little fishing port known throughout Portugal as the country's "octopus capital."

Santa Luzia is not on the open sea but on the channel between the mainland and Tavira Island. Along the waterfront are several seafood restaurants, where you can sit and eat with views of the gulls and the fishing boats moored in the channel and just soak up the atmosphere of a quiet coastal town.

From there, keep following the Ecovia cycle route, which sometimes weaves between saltpans and lagoons and is a great way to see the east Algarve coast. You eventually emerge in the friendly little fishing port of Fuseta where you can catch a train back to Tavira or elsewhere.

*****

Pedals, prawns, and pirates

This tried-and-tested itinerary for exploring the east Algarve coast by bike-train hybrid guarantees you an excellent round-trip day…

Take the train from Vila Real de San Antonio (VRSA) to Fuseta Moncarapacho. You can put bicycles in the car right behind the driver.

From Fuseta, cycle along the Ecovia path in the direction of Tavira, past salt pans with flamingos feeding.

After a bare half hour or so, you will arrive at the splendid seafood restaurant Os Fialhos where some of the tables are right by the lagoon. Try the Algarve oysters and large grilled prawns on skewers with some chilled white wine.

Refreshed, head off again, still in the direction of Tavira. You will pass a 16th-century stone tower, the Torre de Aires, which once served as a watchtower on the lookout for Barbary pirates. Take a little break to admire the little tower and the sea views from here. Dip your feet in the water if you need a quick cool down.

Off again, still following the Ecovia, and you will come to the new settlement of Pedras d'El Rei. From here, it makes sense to switch from the Ecovia to the tarmac road, which follows the line of the lagoons.

Stop for an afternoon drink in the fishing village of Santa Luzia, which describes itself as the Octopus Capital, on account of the local catch, which features prominently on Santa Luzia menus.

From here, it is a short ride on a cycle path to Tavira, where you can catch the train back to VRSA.

*****

⊙ **Vicentine Coast**

Portugal's wildest surf sanctuary

Stretching along Portugal's southwestern coast, about an hour from the southernmost tip, Costa Vicentina Natural Park is a sanctuary for surfers and lovers of wild, rugged natural landscapes. This region boasts dramatic cliffs, golden sandy beaches, and a laid-back coastal lifestyle, complemented by fishing villages and small towns. Enjoy scenic hikes along the cliff tops, discover hidden coves and remote beaches, watch breathtaking sunsets, and experience world-class surfing conditions.

***

Mom-and-pop promenade

The Rota Vicentina in southwest Portugal connects 200 local businesses that created a network of single-track walkable routes accompanied by local cottage industries along the way.

The paths stretch for an incredible 400 kilometers (249 miles), covering two main trails: The Fisherman's Trail and The Historical Way, and eight circular routes, covering a diverse and spectacular landscape.

All the routes are well-marked; the coastal route is marked with blue and green stripes, and the inland route is marked with white and red stripes. All the trails are easy and almost every town on the Rota Vicentina has ATMs, shops, restaurants, and hotels en route.

The Rota Vicentina has an excellent official website to help you plan your visit: https://rotavicentina.com/en/.

***

⦿ Vilamoura

Top place to dock in style

Vilamoura Marina is the largest and the first-ever established marina in Portugal. It's also got a laundry list of recognitions…

The first marina in Portugal to be awarded a Blue Flag, it most recently won the title "International Superyacht Marina of the Year" in 2024. It has taken the award for Best International Marina by The Yacht Harbour Association for years running, and it earned its 13th consecutive Best Portuguese Marina win in 2024. In 2023, it claimed the industry's highest honor, becoming the first Portuguese marina to receive the 5 Gold Anchor Platinum certification. And the list goes on…

Needless to say, if you want to keep a boat in this part of the country, this is the place to come.

***

⊙ Vila Real de Santo Antonio

Best place to see baby flamingos

The Castro Marim reserve, right next to Vila Real de Santo Antonio, is the oldest in continental Portugal and well worth a visit. You can walk or cycle on paths that skirt important wetlands, rich in birdlife, including flamingos. In 2021, the reserve made news because, for the first time, its flamingos raised young on Portuguese soil. According to the government's Institute for Nature Conservation and Forests, about 550 baby flamingos hatched in a colony of about 3,000 birds. Researchers said that a reduced human presence during the COVID-19 pandemic might have been a factor in encouraging the flamingos to breed.

***

Portugal On Two Wheels

Many Portuguese enjoy cycling for fun, but there's also a fiercely competitive element to the sport, which culminates in the Volta a Portugal competition. This annual event occurs over two weeks in August, directly after the Tour de France, and is known internationally as the Grandíssima. Ten stages challenge even the best of riders, and the competition is often called the "fourth Grand Tour."

There are hundreds—perhaps thousands—of cycle routes throughout Portugal, for both cycling and mountain biking. Many routes are flat, although the coastal routes often include hills and forests to climb through. And thanks to the favorable climate, you can cycle here year round.

Remember your puncture repair kit and an emergency spare tube if you're doing self-guided routes, as bike shops are few and far between. And remember that motorists are mostly respectful of cyclists here, but they do have the right of way on the roads.

***

Tracing history through the footsteps of conquerors

With 14 stops throughout the Algarve, the Umayyad Route in Portugal follows the path the Arabs traveled through Iberia, though the trail actually begins in the Far East and crosses Europe before reaching this region.

In Portugal, however, the route begins in Alcoutim, in the north-eastern corner of Algarve, and leads on to Martim Longo, São Bras de Alportel, Estói, Faro, Silves, Monchique, Aljezur, Sagres, Alvor, Vilamoura, Tavira, Cacela Velha, and finally ends in Vila Real de Santo Antonio.

If you're looking for a fun road trip, this is a great itinerary around Algarve.

The Islands

⦿ Madeira

Step into Europe's last ancient laurel forest

The 2-million-year-old Laurissilva Forest in Madeira is a living relic of the ancient laurel forests that once covered large parts of Europe. Designated a UNESCO World Heritage Site, this ecosystem covering over 15,000 hectares—about 20% of the entire island—is completely untouched. The forest is home to an array of flora and fauna and serves as a habitat for endangered bird species. The forest is also characterized by its *levadas*, irrigation channels built centuries ago that now serve as walking trails. Waterfalls, streams, and breathtaking viewpoints are also on the bucket list for visitors.

***

The most finicky viewpoint in Portugal

Pico Ruivo is the third-highest peak in Portugal at 1,862 meters (over 6,000 feet) above sea level, affording amazing views from the top… just make sure it's a cloud-free day when you make the trek. When it's clear, you've got stunning panoramas of not only the peak's island, but also those nearby.

***

Madeira's legendary water walks: The ultimate walk on the edge

The island's *levadas*, irrigation canals that are unique to Madeira, provide a network of about 1,350 miles (over 2,170 kilometers) of built-in routes from the north to the south of the island. Happily for hiking enthusiasts, these also provide man-made walking paths. They can be easy and relaxing walks through the countryside… or they can be narrow, crumbling ledges where a slip could result in injury or death. These are amazing hiking routes, but you'll want to do some research before choosing a path to make sure it's in good condition and accessible.

***

National Bests

Camino de Santiago

The coastal Camino

For the intrepid walker, the Portuguese Camino de Santiago route is the second most popular Camino de Santiago route after the Camino Frances. More than 25% of all pilgrims who arrive in Santiago de Compostela every year arrive via the Portuguese Camino route.

The total distance of the Camino from Porto to Santiago depends on the route you choose: the Coastal Route is 280 kms (174 miles), and the Central Route is 260 kms (162 miles). If you start the Camino in Lisbon, then the total distance to Santiago is 616 kms (383 miles). You can also add on a detour and walk through Fátima, adding about 25 kms (16 miles) to the route.

May and September are the best months to walk the Camino, offering the best weather and fewest pilgrims. July and August are the most popular months, but also the hottest, so most people start out early to avoid the hottest parts of the day.

⊚ Serra Da Estrela Mountain Range

Where Portugal does winter

Rising in Central Portugal, the Serra da Estrela mountain range is home to the highest peak in mainland Portugal, Torre, standing at over 6,500 feet (nearly 2,000 meters) above sea level. Above all, and despite the weather, Serra da Estrela is a unique spot for outdoor enthusiasts, with opportunities for activities like hiking and mountain biking. The region is also renowned for its dramatic valleys, glacial lakes, and traditional mountain villages.

For many Portuguese, this is the go-to place when they want to have some fun in the snow. The most popular ski resort is Estância de Ski da Serra da Estrela, located near the town of Loriga at the top of Torre Mountain. Skiers can choose between 10 runs of varying difficulty, from green to black, covering almost 5 miles (7.7 kilometers). The resort was established in the early 1950s, and they have a comprehensive system of artificial snowmaking in case the real thing is hard to find. There is a mountain restaurant on site and more than a dozen hotels in the vicinity. The center is usually open for four to five months over the winter.

SkiParque Serra da Estrela, also known as the SkiParque Manteigas, not far from the town of Manteigas, is the country's secondary ski resort. A reasonable 25 euros will get you a one-day pass in the peak season. It's only 15 euros in the low season. You can rent everything you need to get you whizzing down the slopes.

7. Sports

Whether you're an armchair enthusiast or a fitness fanatic, there's something sporty for everyone in Portugal. This country offers a wide range of sports and activities that you can either participate in or just watch and enjoy—many of which you might not have known of…

Most folks know about the great golfing—but did you know Portugal offers world-class conditions for many sports, and even holds world records in some cases.

Northern Portugal

⊚ Porto

Where the sand is for spiking

About 25 minutes outside of Porto is the city of Espinho, which is the home of the annual Volleyball Beach Pro Tour and is known as the home of volleyball in the country. The event takes place for a week in June and there is free entry for spectators—a great way to see the game played at the highest level.

Portugal's Other National Sport

Volleyball is a popular summer sport in Portugal, and you'll find large sections of beach roped off for schools and tournaments beginning from April, especially in Algarve.

While some of these are reserved for clubs or schools, many larger beaches have beach volleyball nets set up in the sand, and no one minds if you pick up a ball and start playing.

***

Central Portugal

⊙ Cascais

The capital of clay

Estoril Tennis Club is the epicenter of the sport, and their annual Open Clay Court Tournament attracts international players that rank in the world's top 10. The annual event, part of the ATP Tour, takes place at the sports complex of Clube de Ténis do Estoril in Cascais.

Portugal's Love Affair With Tennis

Tennis is said to be the third most practiced sport in Portugal, no doubt thanks to the mild climate. Being so popular, it's a great way to integrate into a community here. You'll meet locals, other expats, maybe join a club...

Tennis academies abound across the country for budding players, and many resorts have tennis courts and competitions for both residents and vacationers. Some clubs offer a variety of special packages that include accommodation and coaching.

The courts range from all weather, clay, and artificial grass to Canadian clay. Many larger hotels and holiday resorts also have courts or tennis facilities and a number of them can also provide resident coaches, most of which are bilingual or multilingual.

***

A gusty green

If you're in Lisbon, Sintra, or Cascais, don't miss the Oitavos Dunes Course. This is a stunning golf course designed by the highly regarded golf architect Arthur Hills. The 18-hole, par-71 course is beautifully situated on the Lisbon coast, near the Sintra Mountains, overlooking the Atlantic Ocean. The course is characterized by wide sand dunes, and the ocean plays a part in the proceedings, too, adding its gusting Atlantic winds to the mix. Golfers often stay at the luxury Oitavos hotel, which overlooks the fairway and is set amidst outstanding natural beauty.

***

The breeziest bay near Lisbon

Most people head south for boating, but if you're in Lisbon or elsewhere in central Portugal, you're actually close to some of the best sailing conditions in the country. Cascais Bay is a great location for sailors and it's famous for hosting some of sailing's most prestigious events, such as the Tall Ships Race and the Volvo Ocean Race.

*****

⦿ Nazaré

Home of the biggest waves in the world

Simply put, Praia do Norte beach in Nazaré is a record-setting beach, home to the biggest surfable waves in the world.

The reason for the epic waves is an undersea canyon just off the coast, the largest submarine canyon in Europe, reaching depths of about 4,878 meters (16,000 feet) and a length of about 230 kms (143 miles). Because of this fault, waves are able to travel at much greater speed, arriving at the coastline with almost no loss of speed or height, creating the record-breaking waves.

In 2011, Garrett McNamara rode what was then calculated as the biggest wave ever, measured at 23.7 meters (78 feet) and entered the Guinness World Records. In 2017, also in Nazaré, Brazilian Rodrigo Koxa beat him with a ride on a 24-meter (80-foot) wave. And in 2020, the record was smashed once again, with an 86-foot wave that put 37-year-old Sebastian Steudtner into the Guinness World Records for biggest wave ever surfed.

Thus, the marker was set, and Nazaré entered into folklore as "the place" to surf. This is obviously not a beach for beginners, but if you're an experienced surfer—this is the ultimate beach to challenge yourself on.

*****

⦿ Peniche

Top spot to learn surfing near Lisbon

Beginner surfers should check out Cantinho da Baía at Peniche, about an hour north of Lisbon. It's one of Portugal's most consistent and beginner-friendly surf spots, with mellow waves, a sandy bottom, and plenty of surf schools offering lessons and board rentals right on the beach.

If you're feeling more adventurous—or just want to watch the pros in action—head a little further down to Praia dos Supertubos, Peniche's world-famous break that hosts the World Surf League every year. While it's not ideal for beginners to paddle out here, it's a great spot to see how it's done by the best.

Between surf lessons, grab a bite at the beach cafés, stroll along the wide-open sand, or check out the fortress in town. Peniche is a working fishing town with a laid-back vibe and plenty to explore after your surf session.

Surf's Up!

Portugal's huge, 1,794-kilometer (1,115-mile) coastline ensures that surfing is well catered for.

In October 2020, a world-record-breaking wave put 37-year-old Sebastian Steudtner into the Guinness World Records for biggest wave ever surfed. The wave reached 26 meters (86 feet).

The west coast of Portugal is the perfect place to pull out your surfboard and ride some gentle waves. Surf schools abound, and there are locations suitable for everyone from beginners to the more experienced.

⌖ Serra de Estrela

Ski from the highest peak

The most popular resort is Estância de Ski da Serra da Estrela, located near the town of Loriga at the top of Torre Mountain. This is the highest point of mainland Portugal at 1,993 meters (6,539 feet). Skiers can experience 10 tracks of varying difficulty, from green to black, covering almost 5 miles (7.7 kilometers). The resort was established in the early 1950s, and they have a comprehensive system of artificial snowmaking in case the real thing is hard to find.

***

Skiing in Portugal?

Portugal: Home of sunshine, beaches, and bikini-clad vacationers... and snow?

If you love winter sports, there's an option for you in Portugal. Head to the Serra da Estrela, and if you're lucky, and it has snowed enough, you can ski to your heart's content.

Portugal's cheapest lift ticket

If you're looking for a fun day in the snow without breaking the bank, head to SkiParque Serra da Estrela, also known as SkiParque Manteigas, near the mountain town of Manteigas. This is Portugal's most affordable ski experience—and a perfect introduction to snow sports for beginners, families, or casual skiers.

A one-day pass will set you back just 25 euros in peak season, and a mere 15 euros in the low season, making it the best-value slope in the country. The park offers equipment rental on site, and while it's smaller than its big sister resort on Torre Mountain, it provides enough space and terrain for a satisfying day of skiing, sledding, or snowboarding.

And when you're ready for a break, Manteigas itself is a charming village to explore, offering traditional Serra cuisine and warm mountain hospitality.

Southern Portugal

⊚ Alvor

Where the Algarve bowls

One of the biggest lawn bowling clubs in the Algarve is the Alvor Bowls Club. Founded in 1995 by José Martins da Silva, the family-owned club wants to promote lawn bowling as a sport. It has nine rinks and hosts experiences, competitions, tournaments, and social bowls. Annual membership costs 75 euros, and they currently have over 100 members. Visitors pay 10 euros with 2 euros extra to rent equipment.

Lawn Bowling Gains A Following

Currently only practiced in the Algarve, lawn bowling is rapidly increasing in popularity, with several active clubs and with others planned to open in the future.

There are only four members' clubs in the Algarve, where the members actually run and administer the club. Some larger hotels also have greens open to both visitors and locals.

All the clubs welcome visitors from abroad, and many organize holiday tours to the Algarve. Some provide a full range of bowls that can be rented to the visitor at a nominal charge.

⦿ Lagos

A course with a view

The Boavista Golf Course at Praia da Luz is an 18-hole, par 71 championship course with some challenging holes. The golf course provides nice views over the Atlantic Ocean and is surrounded by pine, fig, palm, and olive trees.

***

Wonderful winds on the southern seas

In the south, Lagos claims the top spot for sailing. It's regularly been the venue for international regattas.

Counsel For Captains

Portugal's coast divides into two distinct areas: the west and the south. They are each very different.

The ports on the west coast are situated mostly in estuaries or rivers...

The southern coast, in the Algarve region, can be divided into two parts again: Sotavento, that is sheltered from the wind, and Balavento, that faces the wind.

On this coast, there are several wide, easy-access marinas, making it the more popular choice for boaters in Portugal.

(Warning: Watch out for lobster pots.)

⦿ Odeceixe

Best river-to-ocean paddle in Portugal

Further up the western Algarve coast, the town of Odeceixe, with its wonderful tidal river that winds gently down to the sea, is a great spot for a relaxed paddle. The river provides calm, sheltered waters ideal for kayaking or stand-up paddleboarding, even for beginners. As you glide along, you'll pass through a scenic valley flanked by green hills and whitewashed cottages, with birdlife all around and the scent of eucalyptus in the air. At the mouth of the river, the landscape opens up to reveal Praia de Odeceixe, a stunning beach framed by cliffs—perfect for a post-paddle swim or sunset picnic.

***

⦿ Portimão

A safe haven

Many sail charters leave from Portimão, Lagos, and Vilamoura, and there are a wide range of boats available, but if you're a bit skittish on boating, head for Portimão, which is considered the safest harbor in Portugal.

***

⦿ Praia da Rocha

The most international volleyball beach

In the Algarve, Praia da Rocha is the place to go to watch or play beach volleyball. The annual Deep Dish Portugal Camp sees thousands of players from around the world gather together to enjoy the sport in the sunshine, along one of the widest beaches in the Algarve. The event has training, coaching, competitions, and an end of camp party and awards ceremony. If you're spending time here during this event, prepare to share the town with students from all over the world. These guys work hard and then play hard…

***

Top spot for a cruise departure

If you don't want to take the tiller yourself, buy a ticket and enjoy an organized excursion on an old sailing vessel that meanders lazily along to catch the setting sun, or take a bouncy ride out to a famous landmark like the Benagil Caves, cruise alongside a family of dolphins, or go whale watching along the coast. You can get these kinds of boat excursions from almost any town in the Algarve, but Praia da Rocha is a top spot for departures. WildWatch Tours Algarve, just across the river, prides themselves on their tours, which are guided by marine biologists, and they are keen to promote ecotourism.

***

⦿ Praia do Amado

The Algarve's ultimate wave haven

Wild and unspoiled, this is a magnificent beach to get away from it all with its soft sand and vast skies. The beach is on the west coast near Carrapateira and stretches for over half a mile (almost 1 kilometer). It's a wonder of nature, with incredible cliffs and stunning rock formations.

Amado is an extremely popular spot for surfers. Some even say it has the perfect conditions for surfing. International surfing competitions are held here, and the waves in the winter are amazing. There's also an international surf school here, though it's certainly not suitable for beginners…

It's a beach that never gets crowded, even in summer. The sand is soft and perfect for walking along the water's edge. There are also some fabulous walking trails to discover on the cliffs overhead.

***

⊚ Salema

The course that keeps you coming back

The Golf Santo Antonio is an 18-hole course set within the Parque da Floresta resort. It offers stunning views of fishing villages, the coast, the bucolic scenery, and occasionally the sea. Thanks to its more challenging holes, this is a course even very experienced golfers always want to return to in the hopes of mastering it.

***

The most legendary par 5 in the Algarve

Silves' Pestana Silves Golf Course and its challenging 18-hole, 72-par course just outside the town offer a great challenge for golfers. It's serene but challenging with its arrangement of bunkers, water hazards, and fast greens. It's a great test of golf, and the scenery is stunning. If you play it, watch out for the stunning 12th. To many, it's the best par 5 in the Algarve.

***

⊚ Tavira

The eeriest beachscape with the most secluded sands

Praia do Barril is located on the Ilha de Tavira, just west of the town of Tavira. This beach has a huge stretch of white sand, and you're almost guaranteed some peace and quiet here. Aside from sunbathing, this beach is also a great location for surfing.

The beach is most famous for its Anchor Graveyard or "Cemitério das Âncoras" hidden amongst the dunes. The sight of hundreds of rusting and rotting anchors all lined up in rows is quite something. The area used to be a major tuna fishing area, and the anchors were used to tie the tuna nets in place. With the decline of the industry, they left the anchors to rot, and they are still there to this day.

Just a warning: The western end of the beach is an official nudist beach, but it's well signposted if you're looking to avoid it.

***

The only Nicklaus course in the country

Golf legend Jack Nicklaus is the name behind the Monte Rei Golf Club near Tavira in the eastern Algarve. Only one of a handful of Jack Nicklaus signature courses in Europe and the only one in Portugal, this is an undulating 18-hole, par-72 that has outstanding views all around and some tricky holes to negotiate.

***

⑨ Vicentine Coast

A triple-threat surf series

On the wild and rugged western coast of the Algarve, you'll find a trio of world-class beaches that consistently draw surfers from around the globe. Praia do Amado, often called one of the best surf beaches in Portugal, is known for its reliable waves, dramatic cliffs, and international surf competitions. Just up the coast, Arrifana is a favorite for its crescent-shaped bay, stunning sunsets, and consistent right-handers that appeal to both intermediate and advanced surfers. Further north, Castelejo offers a more secluded surf experience, framed by steep cliffs and backed by raw natural beauty. All three beaches have well-established surf schools and rental shops, making them perfect not only for seasoned wave chasers but also for beginners ready to paddle out for the first time.

***

⑨ Vila do Bispo

Waves and wind, fishing and formations

Near Vila do Bispo in western Algarve, Cordoama is a soft, sandy beach that joins Castelejo beach at low tide. The border between these two beaches forms a series of stunning rock formations, which make for a fascinating beach walk. If you fancy fishing, this is a favored spot for sea anglers. It's also a favorite for surfers and a famous spot for paragliding.

The beach itself is a great destination—it's about half a mile (over 1 kilometer) long, with plenty of space for everyone or any activity. In the winter, it's a popular dog walking destination.

***

⦿ Vilamoura

The pinnacle of Portuguese tennis

One of the largest tennis facilities in the country is the Vale de Lobo Tennis Academy in the Algarve. The Academy boasts a total of 13 courts as well as mini tennis and padel facilities. Open to members and visitors, the Academy runs a busy year-round program of individual and group coaching, tournaments, social match days, and other experiences. The resort has 9 hard courts (4 floodlit), 4 artificial clay courts (all floodlit) and 3 padel courts (all floodlit).

This is the home of Padel Tennis in Portugal and their modern tennis coaching academy offers lessons for tennis stars as young as four years old. The club is a member of both the Portuguese Tennis Federation and the Portuguese Padel Tennis Federation. The club features two acrylic hard-courts, two artificial grass courts, a synthetic clay court, and two state-of-the-art padel tennis courts. Their Academy is the training ground for competition players who train on a daily basis. All levels are catered through a wide range of classes and competitions.

***

The gold standard in Portuguese marinas

Portugal's largest and oldest marina, Vilamoura Marina is also its most celebrated, winning numerous awards, including a Blue Flag, International Superyacht Marina of the Year, Best International Marina, and Best Portuguese Marina for 13 years running. It's also received the industry's highest honor, the 5 Gold Anchor Platinum certification—the only marina in Portugal to do so. And that's just the shortlist. When it comes to boating of any kind, this is the top place to keep a boat in the south.

***

Most photo-worthy course

The most photographed course in Portugal has to be the Vale de Lobo Royal Course, and in particular, its world-famous 16th hole. The cliff-top break in the course is one of the most challenging shots in the country and certainly the most famous. The 18-hole, par-72 Royal Course was designed by Rocky Roquemore.

***

Golf behind the velvet rope

San Lorenzo Golf Course is one of the most popular golf courses in Portugal and is ranked as one of the finest in Europe. It enjoys a magnificent location on the exclusive Quinta do Lago estate in the Algarve.

This 18-hole, par-72 gem is laid out in a figure of 8 with several inland lakes. It is surrounded by woodlands, with views over the Ria Formosa estuary. The 18th hole is renowned for its difficulty. San Lorenzo is available exclusively to guests of the Dona Filipa Hotel, the Amarante Formosa Park hotel, and those folks who are lucky enough to be private members.

***

Europe's Golf Capital

Portugal, and specifically the Algarve, is a golfer's paradise, boasting some of Europe's finest championship courses all set in magnificent surroundings, and many have breath-taking views of the coastline. It's not difficult to see why people like playing golf here.

The mild winter weather in the Algarve meant that golfers could extend their golf season and enjoy their game almost year-round. As a result, a new branch of tourism was born in the region.

***

The grass is always greener—so import it!

The Vilamoura Lawn Bowls Club was established in 1993 and hosts two championship grass greens (with 14 rinks in all). Their greens all have natural grass imported from Oregon State University.

***

The Islands

⊚ Madeira

Best golf on the island

There are three main golf courses on Madeira, but Santo da Serra Clube de Golf in Machico is the firm favorite—home to the Madeira Island Open and widely considered one of the most scenic courses in Europe. Set high in the hills with panoramic views of the Atlantic and rugged coastline, the course offers a mix of dramatic elevation changes and lush fairways that challenge even seasoned players. Designed by Robert Trent Jones Sr., it features 27 holes split into three 9-hole loops, each offering its own unique vistas and test of skill.

***

The farthest fairway in Portugal

Located on the island of Porto Santo, reachable by ferry or short flight from Madeira, this 27-hole course was designed by Severiano Ballesteros. It includes an 18-hole championship course and a 9-hole pitch-and-putt course. The back nine runs along the dramatic coastline, offering breathtaking ocean views and a challenging seaside experience. This has to be one of the most remote, hardest-to-get-to courses in the world…

8. Travel and Transportation

By Road

Driving in Portugal can be a thrilling experience, though it's important to keep in mind that the country has its own unique road culture. Portuguese drivers tend to be fast and aggressive, so it's important to stay alert and avoid distractions while on the road.

However, the well-maintained toll roads and highways make long-distance travel a breeze. With practice and patience, driving in Portugal can become a comfortable part of your visit or your new life here, offering the freedom to explore all that the country has to offer.

However, expect a ton of roundabouts, tight parking spots, and manual cars to be the norm…

***

Keeping It Legal

To legally drive in Portugal beyond the length of your tourist visa or under a different visa after 90 days, you'll need to exchange your current license.

If you're in Portugal as a tourist, you can drive on your current home country's driver's license without concern for 185 days—but only as long as you are in the country on a tourist visa.

For those on a residency visa, you can only use your foreign license for 90 days and be able to exchange it without needing to be tested… however, you have two full years to make the exchange. It's a bit of a bureaucratic conundrum.

If you wait past the two years given for exchange, you'll have to be tested in order to get a local license.

***

The cheapest way from A to B

Buses are a good option for travel around the country, and most journeys will cost you about 5 to 6 euros. A monthly pass will cost you about 40 euros. If you are over 65, you can enjoy bus and train travel for half price.

***

Pay the toll for quality control

Portugal offers pristine toll roads throughout the country, most leading to Spain. These well-maintained highways facilitate easy road trips, while an extensive bus network offers economical options for traveling further afield. You can drive from Lisbon to Porto in just about three hours. Lisbon to Faro in the Algarve in even less time. And Lisbon to Seville, Spain, in under five hours.

***

Skip the line

Having a Via Verde (Green Way) toll tag saves time and hassle when passing through toll booths. If you buy a car and travel beyond your immediate area regularly, it would be worth it to get one.

If you're living in Portugal, have a local bank account, and a locally registered car, the pass is 75 cents per month, plus 32 cents per toll.

If you're just visiting or only have a foreign bank account, it's 1.59 euros per month, and you only pay for the months you're using it.

***

Driver beware

Don't confuse the toll roads with the regional routes. The smaller roads throughout Portugal are not as well-kept as the tollways, and can take much longer to traverse, although they may be more scenic.

***

Best southern workaround

The Algarve has two main roads, the N125, which gets extremely busy in the summer months but is toll-free, and the A22 motorway, which runs from the eastern border with Spain, to just west of Lagos town. If you're here in summer and don't want to sit in traffic, avoid the N125 and opt for the toll road for efficiency.

***

Parking

Sidestep summer struggles in Algarve

In the Algarve, parking ranges from difficult to impossible to find in the tourist season, and few downtown residences offer space for your car. Unwitting tourists sometimes even snag reserved spaces. If you're exploring the region in summer, consider getting a train or bus to your destination and then exploring by foot unless you live in the region and already have a car here… and perhaps even if you do.

***

Primo parking in Coimbra

When driving to Coimbra, park your car in the Santa Clara parking lot, near the bridge with the same name, or in the designated parking spaces by the side of the road, to the left of the bridge.

***

Best lot in Caldas

Rua Rafael Bordallo Pinheiro in Caldas da Rainha is a simple, free open-air parking lot. In the morning, and especially during weekends, it can be full, as many locals like to park there to go to the nearby market (Praça da Fruta).

***

Apps

The cheapest rideshares

Bolt ridesharing service is an equivalent to Uber. It works the same way, through an app, and is usually cheaper.

However, it's also the least well-regulated transport app when it comes to reliability.

You may get your ride without any problems… or you might find that no one arrives… and you may even be told that you're in the car and your ride has begun. You'll have to cancel the ride and go through the system to get a refund (which will almost surely be given, but it's a hassle).

****

Taxis on tap

The best local taxi app is FREENOW, which is Europe's largest multi-mobility app, meaning it offers cars, electric scooters, electric bikes, electric mopeds, and car sharing. It's available in more than 150 cities across 9 European countries. In Portugal, it's the top app for getting a car on demand.

****

Portugal's own taxi service

Taxi-Link is a taxi app that works 24/7 in the main cities of Portugal, working in partnership with the major local taxi fleets. The coverage provided by the thousands of taxis working with them allows a pickup time within minutes.

****

Cashless parking

The Estacionar app connects to your Via Verde toll pass and allows you to pay for parking from your phone, so you never need loose change to pay for parking.

****

Finding your own way

Google Maps and Waze are both used to navigate the local streets and find your way around. Waze is known for its user-sourced input, so, for example, it will warn you about police on the road, speed traps, traffic jams, etc. As a user, you will be asked to contribute.

But be careful, because what these apps consider roads are sometimes nothing more than a trail through the woods… and in very remote areas, they may indicate a route that doesn't exist at all, telling you to drive through a field.

***

Navigating the local networks

Citymapper is a public transit app and mapping service that offers transport options, usually with live timing, between any two locations in a supported city. The key difference between it and Google Maps, for example, is that it specializes in public transport mapping, giving you the best options after taking into account metro, tram, bus, bike, and walking.

***

═══════ By Rail ═══════

Although the rail networks in Portugal don't serve as viable means of international travel—yet—they are excellent for getting across the country.

***

Best deals on wheels

Rail travel is extremely affordable in Portugal, especially long-distance. If you buy your train tickets more than a week in advance, you will get a discount of around 40% to 50%.

***

Capital connections

Gare do Oriente, one of the main train stations in Lisbon, is the easiest to reach by metro from the airport and takes you to both suburban and regional destinations.

Other main train stations include Rossio and Cais do Sodré, which take passengers to Sintra and Cascais, both in the Lisbon Metropolitan Area.

The Santa Apolónia train station connects to other regions in the country.

****

Setting forth for the north

The train is the easiest and most comfy to get from Lisbon to Porto. Especially if you snag business class tickets on one of the direct trains. The regional trains make more stops and therefore take longer. If you're headed straight to Porto, make sure you book the faster service. That business seat on the faster train can run as little as 40 euros without any discounts and takes about three and a half hours. If you book ahead and look for a sale, it could be even cheaper.

****

The far-reaching future

There are currently no direct connecting train routes to Spain, although you can make it work if you cobble together several regional services.

But there are plans in the works for faster trains and high-speed service to Spain. It will be a few more years before we can take advantage of these rail networks, but it's happening.

The high-speed train from Lisbon to Porto is slated to be completed in 2030. And the high-speed route from Lisbon to Madrid in 2034.

By Air

Living in Portugal means you're just a short flight away from some of Europe's most iconic cities and sights. Whether you're planning a romantic getaway in Paris, an ancient adventure in Rome, or a tapas tour in Barcelona, Portugal's proximity to the playground of Europe makes it a very attractive launchpad.

Additionally, the nearby islands of the Azores and Madeira offer unique getaways without even having to leave Portuguese territory.

****

Airport Cheat Sheet

Portugal boasts three major airports: Lisbon, Porto, and Faro. These airports are well-connected to numerous European cities, providing fairly extensive direct flight options and plenty of connecting flights.

In addition, budget airlines like Ryanair, EasyJet, Vueling, and Transavia ensure that travel remains affordable, allowing for spontaneous weekend getaways or planned excursions to major European hubs like Paris, London, Rome, and more. Lisbon boasts flights to 198 global airports by more than 55 different airlines.

***

Taxi alternatives

The Lisbon airport has bus stops connecting to several parts of the city and a direct link to the metro. Gare do Oriente, one of the main train stations in Lisbon, is the easiest to reach by metro from the airport and takes you to both suburban and regional destinations.

***

Help for the handicapped

Portugal's airports offer travelers the MyWay service, which provides personalized assistance for passengers with reduced mobility.

***

The cons of cost cutting

Beware the budget airlines that arrive and depart from Faro in Algarve—they have long check-in queues, so allow extra time to pass through to passport control. Larger airlines, like British Airways, have a smoother and quicker booking-in process. Connections can be made from Faro airport to Lisbon's international airport, which has a much wider choice of onward travel across the world.

***

The ultimate dollar-saving, double-stop deal

Portugal is a great place for a stopover—those elusive deals you can get through your airline where you get to stay in a first location for a week or so before moving on to your final destination. And TAP, its national airline, makes it super simple to do. In fact, TAP's stopover has been voted the best in the world by Global Traveler for years running.

TAP Air Portugal (the national airline) offers a stopover either in Porto or Lisbon. And it's one of the only airlines to offer this on the way to or from your destination (but not both).

As if that wasn't enticing enough, the maximum length of stopover stay time is 10 days—much longer than most airlines offer. Talk about a great two-for-one trip!

Particularly if you're coming from the Americas, Lisbon makes for a wonderful first stop before jetting deeper into the continent and beyond.

***

Island getaways are giveaways

Some of the most consistently cheap flights from Portugal are to the Spanish islands (both Balearic Islands—Ibiza, Mallorca, Menorca—and the Canary Islands), Madrid, London, Toulouse, Lyon, Nice, and Milan.

***

Off-season offers

One perk of living in Portugal and using it as a launchpad to explore Europe is the ability to visit major tourist destinations during non-touristy times. Shorter and cheaper flights (compared to traveling from the States) mean you can choose more selectively when to visit certain hot spots. A quick weekend in Paris, an opera in Milan, or a music festival in Copenhagen on a whim… Europe is your oyster.

***

First choice for Fido

An airline called La Compagnie is a good specialty airline for pets. According to their policy, "small dogs and cats (under 33 pounds, or 15 kilograms) can travel with you in the cabin." Flights land in Paris, so this won't get you all the way to Portugal, but it's a good option for larger dogs to get across the Atlantic.

***

If not by air, then by sea

Cruising across the Atlantic on the Queen Mary II is an alternative to flying with pets. The ship docks in the U.K., though, which requires two weeks of quarantine. Animals must spend the majority of the time in a kennel in a pet-designated area of the ship—so not with you in cabin.

***

Posh pups only, please

Have a large dog or dogs and refuse to put them in cargo? In love with your snub-nosed pooch who isn't allowed to fly commercial?

A Facebook group called "Chartered Air Travel with Pets" was started in 2021 and now has over 50,000 members, all large-dog owners who connect with each other in order to "carpool" chartered flights with their large or snub-nosed animals.

9. Helpful resources

Apps

Communication

The only chat app you need

In Europe, Whatsapp is king, and Portugal is no different.

If there is one app to download and get familiar with before you get to Portugal, it's this one.

From business deals to family conversations, WhatsApp is an integral part of daily life in Portugal. It's estimated that over 90% of Portuguese people have a WhatsApp account and actively use it for communication purposes.

It's the most popular messaging app in Portugal, making it easier to communicate with new friends and colleagues. You'll rarely find someone actually sending SMS messages.

More often than not, if you're looking for a service or help, one of your local friends will recommend a WhatsApp number, not a website. Available across different platforms, such as iOS and Android devices, it's got an easy-to-use interface and ability to send messages quickly and securely.

***

Food delivery at your fingertips

No matter how much we love to eat out, sometimes we all just want to order in and eat on the couch. When you're too exhausted from exploring all day, use Glovo, a food-delivery app similar to Seamless or Grubhub.

***

The expat news lifeline

Algarve Daily News is a news site run by U.K. expats Sue and Chris Englefield. It's a great initiative with a strong presence in the Algarve, and is at the forefront of both local and national news each week.

***

Language Learning

Talk like a local, not like a tourist

Drops is a fun, gamified European Portuguese language-learning app. Similar to Duolingo in format, it offers short, engaging sessions designed to build vocabulary and pronunciation. The big difference? Drops teaches European Portuguese—unlike Duolingo, which only offers Brazilian Portuguese. With sleek visuals, daily streaks, and quick five-minute lessons, it's an easy and enjoyable way to fit language learning into your day. Ideal for travelers, expats, or anyone wanting to sound more like a Lisbon local than a Rio regular.

***

Translation you can trust

DeepL is a powerful translation app often considered more accurate and natural than Google Translate, especially for European Portuguese. Unlike Google Translate, which leans more heavily on Brazilian Portuguese, DeepL provides more contextually appropriate translations for Portugal, making it a top choice for expats, travelers, and anyone learning the language. Its intuitive interface and high-quality output have made it the go-to tool for quick, reliable translations.

***

Multi-function translation

While Google Translate is not the best for European Portuguese translation, it does have some strengths over DeepL, namely its speech-to-text and conversation modes, as well as camera translations (great for menus, signs, labels, etc.). It can also be used offline, which DeepL can't. Those functions mean that aside from just looking up single words or phrases, you can use the audio component to translate your sentences or questions instantly, as well as for those speaking to you. The camera-mode function to hold up your phone to a foreign language sign, menu, book, etc., and see it translated on your screen instantly.

***

Learn At Your Own Risk

Beware of language apps that teach Brazilian Portuguese, like Duolingo.

***

Classes gratis

The PPT Program, Portuguese for All, allows foreign citizens to learn Portuguese at no cost. For official information on Portuguese lessons, check the Instituto Camões website.

Instituto Camões is the official entity regulating Portuguese language learning and examinations, their website (https://www.instituto-camoes.pt/) offers more information on free classes and exams for residency and citizenship.

***

Learn more than just language

Portugueselab.com is a resource for learning Portuguese, this website includes podcasts in European Portuguese in its offerings, making this an informative and multi-educational way to learn Portuguese.

***

Websites

Stay informed in Setúbal

For updated information on events taking place in Setúbal, make sure to keep an eye on the events section of the VisitSetúbal website.

***

For a helping hand

Expat Exchange is a good resource for getting your bearings when you first arrive. This site, with its discussion groups for dozens of individual countries, carries a wealth of information on practical matters from health care to tax.

***

Safe as houses

For advice on protecting property, check out Safe Communities Portugal (SCP), the only national association providing a one-stop-shop for crime prevention and information on security and safety. SCP has several specific safe communities, detailing the services it provides in those areas, including: Safe Communities Algarve, Safe Communities Lisbon, and Safe Communities Madeira.

Newspapers and Magazines

The hub for the grub

Covering Portugal's fabulous food scene from north to south, *Relish Portugal* talks to Michelin-starred chefs, discovers hidden-gem producers, explores unexpected ethnic foods, and showcases emerging and established artists. This award-winning, digital, free-with-subscription, English language food and culture magazine, is a great way to explore the food culture of Portugal.

***

Free paper, valuable info

East Algarve Magazine is an excellent guide to local activities and groups (it's free and widely available in town).

Books on Portugal

Guidebooks And Non-Fiction

A classic for a reason

"Rick Steves Portugal" By Rick Steves: He doesn't just cover the major attractions, he takes you into the small towns and villages, the remote beaches, and the local restaurants and cafés to show you the real Portugal. Top tips, must-see destinations, and clever itineraries will help you pick out the best spots and the most memorable locations of this beautiful country.

***

Discover Portugal through its cuisine

"My Portugal: Recipes And Stories" By George Mendes, Genevieve Ko: Food is one of the best ways to appreciate Portugal. You can enjoy hearty meals sat around the table with family or spend time at a local restaurant sat outside in the sun, enjoying freshly cooked and delicious fish or meat dishes. The Portuguese are proud of their food, and their historic love of travel and exploration has imbibed it with surprising spices and flavors. This book, by renowned chef George Mendes, is full of recipes and stories to inspire you or remind you of your favorite holiday in the sun.

***

Portugal by foot

"Walking Europe's Edge: Reflections On Portugal" By Stephen Powell: This is a fascinating and beautifully written tribute to the people and places of Portugal. From autumn 2018 to spring 2019, Stephen Powell traveled the length of Portugal, following a route of over 930 miles (nearly 1,500 kilometers) on foot. He explored rural landscapes alongside bustling cities, wanting to find the real Portugal beneath the tourist posters. He traveled through almost-extinct rural towns, save for a few old stalwart farming families, and spent time talking to the locals… He intersperses his stories with well-researched and relevant sections covering the history and development of Portugal and its people, alongside traditions and customs. What really stands out about the book is the Portuguese people that he met. Wherever he went, he talked to ordinary folks willing to tell their story to him, and those stories really bring this book to life.

*****

Crash course in language

"First Thousand Words In Portuguese" By Heather Amery: This is a great book to help you learn some basic Portuguese words quickly. It's also in European Portuguese, unlike many other books that cover the Brazilian language (always something to watch out for when you are looking to learn Portuguese). This is a nicely illustrated book with labeled pictures and scenes that help you start to construct basic sentences… and you have the fun of trying to spot the hidden duck on every page, too! The basics in this book are easy to remember and cover most everyday situations.

*****

Next-level lessons

"Practical Portuguese: Language For Living In Portugal" By Sheila Watts: This is a hard book to get hold of but worth hunting down if you want to begin to speak the Portuguese language with some fluency. Sheila moved to live in Portugal in 1987 and found most of the language guidebooks were of little use to her as she tried to navigate her way around the day-to-day reality of living in the Algarve. This is a book for people who live and work here, rather than a phrase book that would help you book a taxi or order food at a restaurant while you are on holiday.

*****

A picture's worth 1,000 words

"Living In Portugal" By Anne De Stoop: This book is a real treat, with sumptuous photography and detailed descriptions… a book to treasure and rest on your coffee table with pride. Portugal is such a beautiful and picturesque place to photograph. This book is a treasure-trove of images and information that will make you want to visit—or even pack your bags and move here.

****

Through the eyes of women

"Women Who Walk: How 20 Women From 16 Countries Came To Live In Portugal" By Louise Ross: This book is a collection of interviews with a diverse group of international women, from a wide range of backgrounds and cultures, who have all made the move to live in Portugal. In 20 different chapters, each woman describes her life story and how she decided to travel and explore the world, each culminating in a move to Portugal. The women describe their wanderlust, the cultural differences they have experienced, and their lives here in Portugal. The book also includes the author's own story of her move to Portugal.

****

Know your history

"The Portuguese: A Modern History" By Barry Hatton: For anyone who wants to know more about Portugal and its people, this is a great modern history book. On the back cover, Hatton says that his purpose in writing this book was to "describe the idiosyncrasies that make this lovely, and sometimes exasperating country unique and to search for explanations, surveying the historical path that drove the Portuguese to where they now stand." Portugal's history is fascinating, and Hatton, who has lived here for many years, is ideally placed to outline the main events in the country's history. He also covers the country's culture and people, including his own personal anecdotes. An interesting and informative book.

****

Portugal versus Spain

"From Gaudí's City To Granada's Red Palace (The Someday Travels Book 2)" By EJ Bauer: This is a charming travel adventure beautifully brought to life. We're sneaking across into Spain for part of this book.

Start and end your travels in Barcelona and enjoy the sights of Spain and Portugal as the author, her sister, and friend travel around these wonderful places together. It's like hearing about a dear friend's latest trip, full of tiny details, shopping expeditions, and historical places. Elizabeth describes things beautifully, whether it's the local food and wine they savor each day, or the little shops full of ceramics and jewelry they just cannot pass by, or the characters they meet on their travels, the author brings them all to life. Fado and Flamenco, azulejos and artisan crafts, city tours, and lots of sparkling glasses of bubbly make this book an entertaining and enjoyable travel memoir.

* * *

Insights from a Nobel-winning local

"Journey To Portugal: In Pursuit Of Portugal's History And Culture" By José Saramago, With Nick Caistor (Translator) And Amanda Hopkinson (Translator): *Readers Digest* invited José Saramago to travel Portugal from north to south, between October 1979 and July 1980. His journey charts a mixture of narratives and memories, legends and myths, as he travels the country, meeting the locals and visiting the villages, towns, and landmarks of Portugal.

José Saramago was born in Portugal in 1922. His work includes plays, poetry, short stories, nonfiction, and seven novels, including "Baltasar and Blimunda" and "The History of the Seige of Lisbon." In 1998 he was awarded the Nobel Prize for literature. His fascination with his country, and especially its people and churches, comes across in this book.

* * *

Portugal in a nutshell

"Moving to Portugal Made Simple" by James Cave: This is comprehensive and well researched—a great starting point. It is available online in paperback and Kindle versions.

* * *

Works Of Fiction Set In Portugal

A great way to complement a trip to Portugal (or anywhere) is to read a good book set in the destination. Whether you're looking for a beach read, historical fiction, surrealism, or just a touching story, finding a fun read will enhance your experience.

***

A proven winner

"Night Train To Lisbon" By Pascal Mercier: This international bestseller is now an award-winning movie. It's a delightful story in which the main character, Mundus, travels to Lisbon to find out more about the enigmatic Portuguese writer, Amadeu del Prado. The history of Portugal, trapped beneath Salazar's dictatorship, makes for an intriguing backdrop to the story. Modern literature at its finest.

***

A twisty thriller

"Two Nights in Lisbon" By Chris Pavone: A woman wakes up to discover her new husband is missing and sets out on a wild race of power, politics, and revenge in this international thriller from *New York Times* bestselling author Chris Pavone. Described as a complex, intelligent, multi-layered thriller, "Two Nights in Lisbon" is filled with twists, turns, husbands, wives, secrets, and lies. The descriptions of Lisbon in the beginning will have you feeling like you're there with the protagonist. And once you get to the end, the story will linger long after you turn the surprising final page.

***

Parallel plotlines spanning the century

"A Small Death In Lisbon" By Robert Wilson: With a dual timeline of 1941 and 1999, this is the story of a German industrialist who moves to Lisbon during World War II and the brutal murder of a young woman along with a police officer. In the late 1990s, investigating the murder of a young girl with a disturbing sexual past, Inspector Ze Coelho overturns the dark soil of history and unearths old bones from Portugal's fascist past. This is an award-winning, fascinating crime fiction book that shows World War II from a different perspective.

***

A dark mystery set in the sunshine

"300 Days Of Sun" By Deborah Lawrenson: A journalist moves to Faro, looking to escape an unsuccessful relationship and a stalled career. She meets a charismatic younger man who begs her to find out the full story of a mysterious child disappearance that happened more than 20 years ago. As a true journalist, she starts investigating, and her search leads her to Ian Rylands, an English expat who cryptically insists she will find answers written in a famous novel. The book recounts an American couple's experience in Portugal during World War II, and their entanglements both personal and professional with their German enemies. Only Rylands insists the book isn't fiction…

***

A quiet but connected community

"Alentejo Blue" By Monica Ali: Famed for her hard-hitting first book, "Brick Lane," this is a much gentler, more passive narrative set in Mamarrosa, a picturesque village in Portugal. It tells the story of a village community through the lives of men and women whose families have lived there for generations. Each character has their own chapter before the final chapter, where a big village gathering brings all their stories together.

***

Surrealism in the serras

"The High Mountains of Portugal" By Yann Martel: The author of the acclaimed "Life of Pi" returns with another faintly crazy novel that centers around a widowed Canadian diplomat who moves to Portugal with a chimpanzee. One character is a man who, thrown backwards by heartache, insists on walking backwards. Another character is a woman who carries her husband to the doctor in a suitcase. Their three stories are intertwined thanks to the discovery of a mysterious journal that leads to an unknown treasure. The book is unique and has been described as "moving, profound, and magical."

***

A soap opera in prose

"The Guilt Trip" By Sandie Jones: Billed as a thriller set in Portugal, this book ends up being more about domestic drama. To celebrate an up-coming wedding, three couples—Jack and Rachel; Noah and Paige; and Will and Ali—have a weekend getaway together. Ali is hiding a secret. And by the end of the weekend, there is one dead body and five people with guilty consciences wondering if they really know each other so well after all.

***

A parallel Portugal

"The Colours of Death" By Patricia Marques: This is crime fiction with a twist. Detective Inspector Reis is in pursuit of a killer. The murders have taken place in an alternative Lisbon where the population is split into gifted or non-gifted. Inspector Reis is registered as gifted as she is a tele-path, which should make her job a lot easier, but the gift comes with its own problems. This is an original crime novel mixed with a hefty dose of science fiction, described as an "amazing genre-bending debut."

***

A serial beach read

"The House that Alice Built" By Chris Penhall: This is book one in the three-part Portuguese Paradise series of lighthearted summer reading. Alice Dorothy Matthews is sensible. While her best friend, Kathy, is living it up in Portugal and her insufferable ex, Adam, is traveling the world, Alice is working hard to pay for the beloved London house she has put her heart and soul into renovating. But then a postcard from Buenos Aires turns Alice's life upside down. One unsensible decision later, and she's in Cascais, and so begins her lesson in "going with the flow." This lesson sees her cat-sitting, paddleboarding, dancing on top of bars, and rediscovering her artistic talents. It's a fun, light-hearted series that will bring the warmth of the Portuguese sun into your life.

Translated Works By Portuguese Authors

From the Renaissance era to modern-day authors and Nobel Prize winners, Portuguese writers have left an indelible mark on the pages of the country's cultural heritage. Getting to know their works will not just inform you on Portugal's culture, history, and heritage, it will also help to familiarize you with names that you'll see again and again as you explore Portugal, as these literary icons are honored and commemorated across the country.

Delve into the richness of their works and explore the legacy they have left on Portuguese literature...

***

The Portuguese Shakespeare

Luís de Camões (1525/26 - 1580) - Renowned writer of the Renaissance era and considered Portugal's greatest poet. Camões is best known for his sonnets and for his epic masterpiece "Os Lusíadas" (The Lusiads). Considered a national treasure, these great epic poems of the Renaissance Period immortalize Portugal's voyages of discovery. First published in 1572, these poems bring to life Vasco da Gama's pioneer voyage via southern Africa to India in 1497 and 1498. The first European artist to cross the equator, Camoes's narrative reflects the novelty and fascination of that original encounter with Africa, India, and the Far East. His lyrical verses and profound themes continue to influence Portuguese literature and culture.

***

The Portuguese Balzac

Camilo Castelo Branco (1825 - 1890) - A prominent novelist of the 19th century, he is well known for his prolific literary work and exploration of complex human emotions, as well as being a crucial contributor to the Romantic movement. Camilo Castelo Branco is best known for his emotionally charged and romantic novels, including "Amor de Perdição"

(Doomed Love).

***

The Portuguese Dickens

Eça de Queirós (1845 - 1900) - A famous writer of the 19th century, he is celebrated for his caustic social satire and realistic portrayals of society. His works, like "Os Maias" (The Maias) and "O Primo Basílio" (Cousin Bazilio), deliver incisive social commentary, often critiquing the moral and social decadence of Portuguese society during his era.

***

The Portuguese Proust

Fernando Pessoa (1888 - 1935) - A highly influential poet and writer, Pessoa is recognized for his innovative use of heteronyms—distinct literary personas with individual voices and personalities. His works, including "The Book of Disquiet" and a vast collection of poetry and prose, reflect his profound introspection, existential themes, and contributions to the modernist literary movement, making him a literary icon in Portuguese and world literature.

***

The Portuguese Plath

Florbela Espanca (1894 – 1930) - This early 20th-century poet became known for her profoundly emotional and confessional poetry, which explores themes of love, passion, and inner turmoil. Her works, including "Livro de Mágoas" (Book of Sorrows), have left a lasting impact on Portuguese literature, and she is celebrated for bringing a distinctly feminine voice to the literary landscape of her time.

***

The Portuguese Heaney

Sophia de Mello Breyner Andresen (1919 – 2004) - A highly esteemed poet and writer, celebrated for her lyrical and introspective poetry, which often draws inspiration from nature, mythology, and history. Her works, such as "O Nome das Coisas" (The Name of Things), are characterized by a deep sense of lyricism and a dedication to exploring timeless topics, earning her recognition as one of Portugal's most influential literary voices of the 20th century.

***

The Portuguese Kafka

José Saramago (1922 – 2010) - Acclaimed novelist and Nobel laureate who is praised for his thought-provoking and innovative literary works, such as "O Evangelho segundo Jesus Cristo" (The Gospel According to Jesus Christ). His distinct narrative style, characterized by long sentences and philosophical reflections, together with his challenge of conventional storytelling and profound philosophical and social questionings, has left an ongoing impact on contemporary literature.

***

The Portuguese Falkner

António Lobo Antunes (1942 -) - Distinguished novelist known for his deeply introspective and often fragmented narrative style, exploring the complexities of human relationships and the lingering traumas of Portugal's colonial past. With notable works like "O Manual dos Inquisidores" (The Inquisitors' Manual), he has earned his reputation as a gifted storyteller and a leading figure in contemporary Portuguese literature.

***

The Portuguese Woolf

Lídia Jorge (1946 -) - A former teacher, her work is aligned with the style of the so-called postcolonial generation of novelists, while also having a strong focus on the social and cultural condition of women. "O Vale da Paixão" (The Painter of Birds) is one of her best-known books, although she has received numerous prestigious prizes for her body of work.

***

The Portuguese Marquez

José Luís Peixoto (1974 -) - Contemporary author, celebrated for his evocative and lyrical prose, often weaving intricate narratives that delve into themes of identity, memory, and human relationships. His novels, including "Cemitério de Pianos" (The Piano Cemetery), reflect his deep connection to the Portuguese landscape and have gathered critical acclaim both in Portugal and internationally.

The Best Of Portugal
For The Retiree

1. Top Destinations To Begin The Hunt For Your New Dream Home In Portugal

It's hard to name the best place(s) in Portugal to retire to—there are just too many! That hasn't stopped us from trying over the last decade or so, though, and the southern Algarve region as well as the areas around Lisbon are always top performers…

But you'd be doing yourself a disservice if you limited your exploration to just these two regions.

In this section, we'll take a look at just a handful of some of our favorite places in Portugal, from the well-known to the never-visited.

Consider this list a starting point for your scouting trips… but remember that it's only meant to be a quick introduction to each, and that you should dig even deeper—and visit in person, of course—to get to know these places and what lies beyond them…

Northern Portugal

⊙ Aveiro: Venice of Portugal

The town of Aveiro, situated on the west coast a little less than an hour's drive from Porto, is known as the Venice of Portugal thanks to its network of canals navigated by gondola-like boats known locally *as barcos moliceiros.*

With uninterrupted sea views and an abundance of fresh sea air, this city is emerging as a top option for anyone looking for a calm and peaceful pace of life in the Old World.

Aveiro is also refreshingly affordable, offering big-city amenities at a nice discount to costs in Lisbon and Porto.

The area is popular for its fresh fish, grilled mackerel, and gastronomic diversity. A three-course meal can cost as little as 7 or 8 euros in a midrange restaurant.

Aveiro is also relatively flat and low-lying, making it an ideal city for walking and biking. Everything is within easy strolling distance of everything else; sidewalks are wide, footpaths in good condition, and many areas pedestrianized.

This city is definitely a good option for someone with mobility re-strictions.

Neighborhoods are small, and locals are friendly. On nearly every corner is a tiny bakery, café, or minimarket, and shopkeepers will know your name after just a week or two.

Aveiro is never as hot as Lisbon, and the sun shines a little less often.

Be sure to appreciate the town's fantastic architecture. Wander through the city center and admire the Art Nouveau architecture, char-acterized by intricate designs and decorative elements. The area is also known for its *moliceiro* boats, the local traditional boats, painted with colorful (and often cheeky) drawings, which are now used to take tour-ists along the city's canals.

And while here, take a detour to Costa Nova, a fishing village that's famous for its striped, candy-colored houses. Take some time to stroll along the boardwalk and visit the beach.

***

⦿ Braga: Stronghold of the Minho

Braga, in the far north of Portugal, is one of Europe's oldest munici-palities. It has been a city for over 2,000 years. This city is in the center of the lush, green Minho region of northern Portugal. It's famous for its historical buildings, monuments, gardens, and fountains.

Here, religious devotion, evident in the many churches and symbols of faith, juxtaposes a modern city, complete with restaurants and bars. Braga is known for its nightlife, thanks in part to the local universities.

Braga has long been a religious center. Pilgrims have journeyed here for centuries. It officially became the religious capital of Portugal in the 12th century. The city dates back to 296 BC, when it was founded by the Carthaginians. The Romans called Braga "Bracara Augusta." Today, it features landmarks in a range of architectural styles. Its unique histor-ical and cultural past have been well-preserved. Local laws put height restrictions on new buildings to preserve the ancient beauty.

The pedestrian area of Braga is extensive. Blocks are filled with bou-tiques, shops, pharmacies, supermarkets, restaurants, cafés, businesses, hotels, homes, apartments, hospitals, churches, gardens, fountains, the-aters… all housed in a magnificently restored area of town.

***

⦿ Cascais: Suburb with style

Originally a small fishing village, caught between the Atlantic Ocean and the waterfront area leading back to Lisbon, Cascais is now sometimes referred to as the Portuguese Riviera. This little city has grown into a popular tourist destination and home to many Portuguese nationals as well as expats from all over the world.

Some of the country's wealthiest and most famous citizens call Cascais home, including the President of Portugal and Cristiano Ronaldo, when he's not scoring goals in professional soccer leagues.

Offering innumerable amenities, fantastic restaurants, tons of culture, gorgeous scenery, and more, you'd be hard-pressed to find a Portuguese city more liked by long-time locals and newbies alike.

With several beautiful beaches within walking distance from the train station, it's an easy beach day out from Lisbon.

And with cultural and entertainment events happening often, more and more restaurants opening, and the fact that Cascais tops list after list of best places to live and visit in Portugal, you're more likely to encounter crowds than not during the high season.

Cascais has all the luxuries of any other urban area—well-maintained roads, reliable electricity, good tap water, high-speed internet (Cascais also offers slow but free city-wide Wi-Fi), a wide-ranging public transportation system, and more.

The city is quick to fix potholes and damaged public spaces, prides itself on keeping the beaches and Paredão clean and safe, and beautifies itself at every opportunity.

While there is a lot of construction happening, the crews work quickly and efficiently, and the city always makes sure to leave an area nicer than they found it.

✳✳✳

⦿ Douro Valley: Portuguese Napa Valley

The Douro region, a UNESCO World Heritage Site, is noted for its stunning landscapes and terraced vineyards that produce the world-famous Port wine. As you navigate the winding roads along the hillsides, you'll be treated to views of lush vineyards, picturesque towns, and serene waters.

A boat cruise along the Douro River is a great way to begin to explore this area—you'll admire the landscape and discover treasures along the way. The region's wine estates offer immersive experiences where you can learn about the winemaking process, sample wines, and indulge in regional cuisine.

Life in the Douro moves at a gentle pace, shaped by the rhythm of the seasons and the grape harvest. Local communities are small and intimate, with an emphasis on traditional values, hospitality, and a deep connection to the land. It's a place where meals are long, wine is central to any gathering, and sunsets over the valley are daily rituals. Whether you're staying in a restored *quinta* (wine estate), enjoying farm-to-table cuisine, or taking part in the grape harvest (*vindima*), the Douro lifestyle is about slowing down and savoring the moment.

***

⊚ Esmoriz: Sea and city

With its beautiful sandy beaches and wonderful surfing conditions, Esmoriz attracts both beachgoers and water sports enthusiasts seeking a relaxing seaside spot. The town has a laid-back, small-town atmosphere with a tight-knit local community. Its lively summer season brings beach bars, open-air concerts, and surf schools to life, while the rest of the year offers a quieter pace, ideal for long coastal walks, cycling, or simply enjoying a coffee at a beachfront café. Just 30 minutes south of Porto, Esmoriz strikes a balance between peaceful living and easy access to city culture and amenities—making it a popular choice for both weekenders and year-round residents looking for a relaxed coastal lifestyle.

***

⊚ Espinho: A shore bet for fun

Known among beach lovers, Espinho is also sought after by surf enthusiasts, even hosting surf competitions. The casino and open-air market are among the local favorites.

Life in Espinho blends laid-back coastal living with vibrant local culture. Mornings often begin with a stroll along the beach promenade or a coffee at one of the seaside cafés. Residents enjoy an active lifestyle—surfing, cycling, and jogging along the coast are part of the daily rhythm. The weekly open-air market, one of the largest in Portugal, is more than a shopping destination, it's a community hub where locals catch up over fresh produce, textiles, and baked goods.

Evenings are lively but never hectic, with families, retirees, and young creatives mingling at beach bars or attending cultural events hosted at the local arts center. It's a place where tradition meets a youthful, surf-town vibe—making Espinho as much about community as it is about the coast.

*****

⊚ Ílhavo: Where sea meets ceramics

A coastal town with a rich maritime heritage, Ílhavo is known for blending history, craftsmanship, and ocean culture. When in Ílhavo, make sure not to miss a visit to the Vista Alegre museum—connected to the high-end ceramics and crystalware brand bearing the same name—and the iconic Praia da Barra, with its lighthouse, the tallest in the country.

Life in Ílhavo flows at a relaxed pace, shaped by both its fishing roots and its strong artistic tradition. Locals take pride in their connection to the sea, with fresh seafood available daily at neighborhood markets and fish restaurants that are beloved gathering spots. The community values craftsmanship, and the influence of Vista Alegre is felt not just in the museum but in the creative spirit of the town—from design workshops to small artisan studios.

The coastal lifestyle here is deeply restorative. Residents enjoy weekend walks or bike rides along the canals of nearby Aveiro, sunset watching at Praia da Barra, and sailing or kayaking on the lagoon. Ílhavo manages to feel authentic and grounded, with a small-town charm that attracts both families and creative professionals looking for inspiration by the sea.

*****

⊚ Porto: Capital of the North

Globally known for its exquisite port wine and surrounded by the enchanting Douro Valley, Porto is Portugal's second city. Considered one of the country's most charming cities, its die-hard fans swear by Porto's exquisite allure and claim it as the city of cities, with a grace beyond compare.

Known as the capital of the north, Porto is a wonderfully central spot to explore all the northwest parts of Portugal, cities like Braga and Guimarães, the banks of the Douro River, and the national park of Peneda-Gerês, and more are easy to reach. Many people who walk the Portuguese Camino de Santiago start their itinerary here.

Even though Porto is smaller than Lisbon, it's packed with services, it has solid infrastructure, and it offers never-ending things to do, see, and enjoy. Art, impressive architecture, historical neighborhoods, beaches, parks, and gardens are some of the perks of this city—and port, of course. Don't forget about port wine.

This illustrious centuries-old fortified wine is produced along the margins of the Douro River, but in Vila Nova de Gaia, literally in front of Porto, you'll find plenty of cellars where you can do wine tastings.

Parque Da Cidade, the city park, is a green paradise in the middle of a busy urban jungle… Bordered by the sea on one side and punctuated by peaceful lakes, the park is home to a stunning variety of local flora and fauna. It has groves, forests, and huge expanses of grassy areas, as well as refreshment stops and picnic tables.

Aliados Avenue and its surroundings are said to be perfectly representative of Porto. Totally refurbished a few years ago, this boulevard is home to the city's most ornamental buildings—and the most beautiful McDonald's in the world, according to *Business Insider*.

Porto combines dazzling urban landscapes, plus the services and infrastructures of a city, with the tradition and proud authenticity of a not-so-big city. The warmth of the people of Porto makes up for the city's slightly colder temperatures.

Santa Catarina Street is mostly pedestrianized and one of the busiest streets in Portugal, and the most commercial artery of the Baixa zone (downtown area). Famous for being the main open-air shopping center in Porto, it is also renowned for its stunning Christmas-light displays during winter and for its beautiful tiles and iconic façades—fine examples of Art Nouveau style. Extending for nearly a mile, this is the largest shopping area in Porto, running from Via Catarina to one of the most well-preserved treasures of Porto, the Majestic Café.

Central Portugal

⦿ Almada: Sea, sun, and a side of Lisbon

Nestled on the banks of the Tagus River, to the south of Lisbon, lies Almada. Almada has long been an appealing municipality, thanks to its many perks: key geographical location, stunning coastal areas (which include about 10 miles of beach area), mild climate, and excellent accessibility. It tends to be a bit warmer and sunnier here than in Lisbon, but the winter months are not without the risk of storms.

In the past few years, the numbers of expats in the English-speaking community have gone up.

Almada is perfect for beach lovers who like to have a more relaxed lifestyle but also treasure being close to the capital and what it has to offer. Other pros include a relatively cheaper cost of living when compared to Lisbon, good public transportation, and a sense of community.

***

⦿ Caldas da Rainha: Where the water heals and the pottery reveals

Famous for its thermal springs, prominent historical buildings, and Bordalo Pinheiro ceramics, Caldas da Rainha is also close to some of the best beaches in the region.

Caldas da Rainha's historical center is where you'll find the market, a main garden or park with a children's playground, a major museum, and at least a handful of good cafés, restaurants, and shops.

The town was founded by Queen Leonor (Rainha Dona Leonor) in 1484 after she saw some peasants bathing in foul-smelling waters by the roadside, claiming the waters had healing properties. Bathing here, she found relief from an unknown illness she had been suffering from, so she ordered the construction of a hospital at the site so that others could benefit as well. To fund the hospital and its adjacent church, the queen sold her jewels and used revenue from her landholdings.

The settlement that developed around this site was named Caldas da Rainha, which translates to "Queen's Hot Springs," honoring both its founder and its origin. To this day, the queen remains a much-beloved figure in Caldas. In the 19th and early 20th centuries it was fashionable to visit thermal bath resorts, and Caldas da Rainha was favored by the aristocracy and the upper classes.

This is also when the town made a reputation for itself for its ceramics. This was largely due to the work of Rafael Bordallo Pinheiro and his brother Feliciano, who established a factory now called Faianças Artísticas Bordallo Pinheiro.

The factory produces a variety of items, from large decorative pieces to tableware resembling fruits, vegetables, and animals, and figurines of Zé Povinho, a caricature of the Portuguese peasants (a Portuguese equivalent of sorts of the British John Bull or the American Uncle Sam).

You may have come across the name Bordallo II, a globally renowned artist known for his creations of large-scale animals made from trash. As you may have guessed from the name, he is the grandson of Bordallo Pinheiro.

It was also in the 19th century that Caldas started making (and being famous for)... ceramic phalluses! What started as a joke became one of the main items the town is known for to this day.

A little-known fact about Caldas is that during World War II (in which Portugal remained neutral) the town welcomed hundreds of Jewish refugees and even set up an improvised synagogue.

Also at this time, over 200 British nationals, most of whom were over 65 years old and who had been living in Italy, were evacuated to Caldas, where they were expected to stay until the end of the war.

***

⊚ Coimbra: City of students

Coimbra, one of the oldest cities in Portugal, is famous for its university, one of the oldest in the world. This UNESCO World Heritage site (also said to have been an inspiration for J.K. Rowlings' Hogwarts), as well as the Santa Cruz Monastery, resting place of the country's first kings, are the top draws here. The Gothic and Manueline architectural elements of the 12th century monastery are reason enough to visit by themselves.

But the city of students, as it's known in Portugal, has several perks that make it the right fit for a growing number of expats.

Coimbra is the capital city of the district bearing the same name and is one of the most important cities in Central Portugal. The city itself has a lot going on, but at the same time, it has a relaxed pace, especially when compared to Lisbon and Porto.

Coimbra comes with its own set of monuments and unique cultural traits, like a specific type of fado (a Portuguese music genre). The natural buzz of the university and the students, creates a fertile ground for exhibitions, concerts, and culture in general. But there's more to it: its central location on the Portuguese map makes Coimbra an ideal location if you plan on exploring the country either for leisure or for work. The city is also home to the Coimbra University Hospital, one of the biggest in the country.

Coimbra is also home to the Machado de Castro National Museum with a great collection of Portuguese art and archaeological findings, but which also offers great views of the city. The building itself is a mix of architectural styles: Roman foundations, a main building that was the bishop's official residence from the 12th to the 18th centuries, and contemporary elements that come together to create the museum space.

Being home to its own unique type of fado, there are several places in the city where you can enjoy small concerts. Keep an eye on the city hall's website for regular updates on cultural events.

There are no particularly good or bad times to visit Coimbra, but you might avoid the second half of May, particularly during the weekend. That is when students celebrate the Queima das Fitas (literally, "burning of the ribbons"), marking the end of their degrees.

Coimbra has the mix of services and historical charm that most Portuguese cities have to offer, but property here manages to be cheaper than in Lisbon and Porto.

The city has an efficient public transportation system with easy connections to both the area around it and to other cities in the country. The student culture is synonymous with a fairly big offering in terms of restaurants, bars, and cultural events. The mild weather is the icing on the cake.

If you love the idea of living in a city that's not too big and not too small, not too busy and not too sleepy, then Coimbra may be the balance you're looking for.

✳✳✳

⦿ Comporta: Martha's Vineyard of Portugal

If you're interested in design and architecture, don't miss Comporta, across the estuary from Setúbal and known for being home to names like Philippe Starck and Christian Louboutin, among others. Once a sleepy fishing village surrounded by rice paddies and pine forests, Comporta has quietly become a haven for artists, creatives, and well-heeled bohemians seeking a slower, more intentional pace of life.

Despite its glamorous reputation, the Comporta lifestyle is more about barefoot luxury than flashy displays. Days here often begin with morning yoga, followed by beachside lunches of grilled fish and chilled white wine. The sandy, windswept beaches stretch for miles and are rarely crowded—even in high season. Design lovers will find inspiration everywhere, from understated architectural villas that blend into the landscape to stylish boutiques, concept stores, and laid-back cafés.

The community tends to be international but low-key, with a shared appreciation for nature, wellness, and good taste. Residents and regulars often get around by bike, shop at local organic markets, and host sunset dinners with long tables set in the dunes. With its blend of rustic charm and minimalist sophistication, Comporta is effortlessly chic, serene, and quietly exclusive.

***

⊚ Figueira da Foz: Queen of the Silver Coast

Located at the mouth of the Mondego River, Figueira is known as the Queen of the Silver Coast. The surrounding natural landscapes—including what is probably the widest beach in Europe—its historical buildings, and the glamorous casino are this queen's crown jewels.

Figueira da Foz offers a unique mix of classic seaside charm and vibrant urban life. The lifestyle here is relaxed yet active, with plenty to do for both locals and visitors. The long, flat promenade is perfect for cycling, jogging, or an evening stroll, often leading to beachfront cafés where you can enjoy a coffee or fresh seafood while watching the sunset over the Atlantic. The beach itself is ideal for families, sunbathers, and surfers alike, with designated zones for water sports and lounging.

The town comes alive in the summer with festivals, outdoor concerts, and cultural events, particularly around the historic Bairro Novo district, known for its art deco architecture and lively atmosphere. Figueira's famous casino is not just a spot for gaming, but also a venue for live shows and upscale dining, adding a touch of glamour to coastal life.

Locals value leisure and community here—weekends are for picnicking in Serra da Boa Viagem or browsing the local markets. And while it's

a popular tourist destination, Figueira retains an authe
feel, with traditional pastry shops, bookshops, and a rh
invites you to slow down and stay a while.

***

⊚ Nazaré: Town with biggest waves in the world

Once a humble fishing village, Nazaré is now internationally re-nowned for its colossal waves and the daring surfers who ride them. Yet, it still proudly celebrates its traditions, from the colorful fishing boats lining the beach to the iconic Nazarenas—local women in their traditional seven-layered skirts, often seen selling dried fish along the promenade.

Life in Nazaré offers a mix of old-world charm and modern-day adrenaline. While the surf crowd flocks here in winter to witness (or brave) the towering waves at Praia do Norte, the rest of the year is a calmer affair, with long beach days, seafood dinners, and seaside strolls defining the rhythm of local life.

Locals and expats enjoy a relaxed coastal lifestyle—mornings often begin with a walk along the promenade or a coffee at a terrace café, with the ocean always in view. The town's fresh seafood is a point of pride, particularly the dried fish still prepared in the traditional way on wooden racks. Nazaré's central market is a hub of daily life, where residents buy local produce, cheese, and fresh-caught fish.

Above town, the cliffside neighborhood of Sítio offers breathtaking views, a funicular ride, and quieter streets lined with chapels and souvenir shops. The lookout point, Miradouro do Suberco, offers a dramatic panorama of the coastline and crashing waves below.

Though Nazaré gets its fair share of visitors, it has maintained its small-town feel and strong sense of community. Whether you're here for the surf, the seafood, or the simple seaside lifestyle, Nazaré has a deep cultural heartbeat that pulses far beyond the waves.

***

⊚ Mira: Traditional fishing village on the Silver Coast

Well known for its spotless beaches and natural beauty—including the serene Lagoa de Mira—this charismatic coastal town retains all the charm of a traditional fishing village. Praia de Mira holds the rare distinction of having flown the Blue Flag for over 30 consecutive years, making it one of the most pristine and acclaimed beaches in the country. The placid lagoon is perfect for kayaking, paddleboarding, or simply soaking in the tranquil scenery.

Life in Mira moves at a gentle, steady rhythm. Locals often begin their day with a stroll or bike ride along the wooden boardwalks that wind between the beach and the lagoon. Many of the colorful wooden homes near the waterfront—some once used to store fishing gear—have been converted into vacation cottages or small cafés, adding to the village's charm without compromising its authenticity.

Freshly caught fish is a staple on every menu, and family-run restaurants serve traditional dishes with a focus on simplicity and flavor. Weekly markets sell local produce, handmade goods, and freshly baked bread. In the evenings, it's not uncommon to find groups of residents chatting in the main square while children play nearby.

Mira is also proud of its heritage. Traditional boats still dot the beach, and fishing remains a core part of the community's identity. Festivals, especially those celebrating maritime culture and local saints, bring together generations and showcase folk music, dance, and regional cuisine.

Though it attracts its share of summer visitors, Mira has remained unspoiled and deeply local—a place where you come for the beach, but stay for the lifestyle.

✳✳✳

⊙ Leiria: City of the castle

In Leiria, the majestic 12th-century castle dominates the skyline, its ancient walls offering sweeping views over the city and surrounding countryside. Classified as a national monument, the castle is not only a historical centerpiece but also a cultural hub, often hosting concerts, exhibitions, and open-air cinema nights during the warmer months.

At the heart of town, Praça Rodrigues Lobo buzzes with local life. This charming square is where friends gather for coffee or an evening glass of wine, families enjoy weekend strolls, and visitors soak up the rhythm of daily life. Lined with a mix of traditional and modern cafés, restaurants, and bookstores, the square serves as the city's informal living room—equal parts relaxed and lively.

Leiria is also a city with a youthful and creative spirit, thanks in part to its vibrant university community. This energy is reflected in the city's celebrated street art, with colorful murals and imaginative facades tucked around nearly every corner. Wandering through Leiria becomes an open-air gallery experience, where urban creativity meets medieval heritage.

The city hosts frequent cultural events, including music festivals, food fairs, and craft markets that highlight local artisans and producers. The Mercado de Sant'Ana, housed in a beautiful old convent, now serves as a cultural venue where locals attend exhibitions, talks, and performances.

Lifestyle here strikes a rare balance—Leiria is big enough to offer the conveniences and cultural buzz of a city, but small enough to retain a relaxed, neighborly vibe. With great food, affordable living, a walkable center, and easy access to both the coast and the mountains, Leiria is a quiet gem in central Portugal that blends old-world charm with modern living.

***

⦿ Lisbon: Noble And Elegant

Lisbon, capital of the country on the Tagus River, is one of the oldest cities in Western Europe, originally settled as a Phoenician trading post. It was in the 15th and 16th centuries, though, that Lisbon flourished. Awe-inspiring landmarks were constructed during this Golden Age of Discovery—the Jerónimos Monastery and the Tower of Belém, for example, and, on the waterfront, the Praça do Comércio. Lisbon became Lisbon thanks to its strategic geographic position at the mouth of the Tagus River. According to a popular fado, Lisbon has always been in love with her river... because the river is the city's lifeline to the sea... and Portugal very much identifies herself with the sea.

Lisbon is a noble and elegant city, one of Europe's least appreciated. Its centuries-old, pastel-colored stone structures are bordered by jacaranda trees and set off by formal gardens and parks with elaborate fountains. Roads, walkways, and pavements are laid with small cobblestones in contrasting colors to create elaborate patterns and sea scenes that are like works of art, almost mosaics.

The broad, placid waters of the Tagus River remain Lisbon's foreground, but beyond now stands the finest of Pombal's colonnaded squares known as the Praça do Comércio, or Black Horse Square, after the equestrian statue of King Jose I in its center. Locals call it the Terreiro de Paço. One magnificent square, among the finest in the world, with three names. From here, two broad avenues lead through the city's principal restaurant and shopping area to another fine square known as the Rossio.

From that point, the broad Avenida da Liberdade, the city's principal artery, climbs straight for over a mile to a big public park named after Britain's King Eduardo VII. Well shaded by trees from the summer sun, it offers strollers broad sidewalks decorated with intricate mosaics of tiny black and white stones carefully tapped into place by an army of municipal workers. Rickety varicolored old wooden trams ply the streets along with open horse-drawn *fiacres*. Kiosks offer alcoholic beverages and sweet treats.

Looking down over Lisbon's agreeable center from the east is the city's Romanesque cathedral, standing on a rocky summit amid the ruins of St. George's Castle. Although badly damaged in the earthquake of 1755, it has been expertly restored and contains a magnificent organ with rows of golden trumpets facing each other across the nave.

Below the cathedral and close to the river's edge is a portion of old Lisbon that escaped the earthquake's shock, the medieval Alfama. It is a sharp reminder of the four centuries Lisbon spent under Moorish rule until captured by King Afonso I in 1147, a neighborhood of narrow, winding streets, frequent flights of stairs, and tall, white Arabian buildings.

The site of a fish market in the morning, at night Alfama becomes the place to dine in its many little restaurants while listening to singers clad in long black gowns chanting the traditional sad Portuguese folk songs known as fado, or fate.

West from Black Horse Square is the Jerónimos Monastery, the finest surviving example of the typically Portuguese Manueline Gothic style, featuring elaborately decorated arches and pillars with nautical motifs.

Living in Lisbon, you have easy access to all sorts of leisure facilities, from museums and art galleries to sports, volunteer groups, libraries, and bookshops. In terms of restaurants, clubs, and nightlife in general, there's also plenty to choose from.

Lisbon is a city of contrasts: urban sophistication blended with sleepy town life, historical districts mixed with modern architecture, a never-ending dance between old and new with deep blue skies watching over everything.

One of the biggest focuses for Lisbon's future is on making the city greener. This means more roads closed to traffic, 10.5 miles of new bike lanes (added to the existing ones), and continuing work on the new Parque Urbano Gonçalo Ribeiro Telles, a green area that will connect to the iconic Gulbenkian gardens. New buses and trams as well as health care units are also in the works.

You'll find small gardens spread around the city: some are a remnant of late 19th century-style public gardens (like Jardim da Estrela), while others have a more modern approach (like Jardim do Campo Grande).

The iconic Gulbenkian Garden, covering an area of around 22 acres (9,000 square meters), is one of the most beloved in the city. Many of these gardens will have a playground and at least one small café with seats outside.

***

📍 Peniche: Surfer's paradise

Home to the world-renowned Supertubos beach—famed for its fast, barreling waves—Peniche is a must-visit destination for surfers from around the globe. But this seaside town offers more than just epic breaks. Nearby beaches like Baleal and Lagide cater to a range of skill levels, and the town has become a vibrant surf hub, filled with surf schools, laid-back beach bars, and a strong sense of community among locals and visiting wave-chasers alike.

Life in Peniche is deeply tied to the ocean. It's still one of Portugal's most active fishing ports, and the daily catch shows up in delicious form at local seafood restaurants. Try the *caldeirada* (a hearty fish stew) or freshly grilled sardines while watching the sunset over Cabo Carvoeiro's dramatic cliffs.

Beyond the waves, Peniche offers a relaxed, coastal lifestyle with a down-to-earth vibe. The whitewashed houses, quiet cobbled streets, and traditional cafés create an unhurried atmosphere that appeals to artists, digital nomads, retirees, and families looking for a more affordable seaside escape.

It's also just a quick ferry ride to the Berlenga Islands, a UNESCO Biosphere Reserve located about 6 miles offshore. The island's crystal-clear waters, seabird colonies, and 17th-century fortress provide a stunning backdrop for hiking, snorkeling, or simply soaking up the solitude.

With its mix of natural beauty, adrenaline-pumping surf, and old-world charm, Peniche is a place where salty hair, seafood dinners, and sunset strolls become part of everyday life.

***

⊚ **São Martinho do Porto:** Easygoing escape by the bay

A charming coastal town famed for its naturally shell-shaped bay, calm waters, and lovely promenade—making it one of the safest and most family-friendly beaches in Portugal. The sheltered bay is ideal for swimming, paddleboarding, and kayaking, with plenty of cafés and restaurants lining the scenic walkway.

The lifestyle in this historical town is all about slowing down. Mornings start with fresh bread from the local bakery, afternoons are often spent lounging by the beach or chatting with neighbors at the *pastelaria*, and evenings bring families and friends out for strolls along the promenade. The town is popular with both Portuguese families and expats, particularly retirees, who are drawn to its walkability, relaxed pace, and sense of community.

Locals gather at the daily market for fresh produce, fish, and flowers, and there's a surprising variety of restaurants—from casual seafood grills to international cuisine. It's the kind of place where time feels like it stretches out, where people remember your name, and where the beach is never more than a few minutes away. Despite its popularity in summer, it retains a tranquil, welcoming atmosphere year-round.

***

⊚ **Setúbal:** Princess of the Sado

Setúbal, known as the princess of the Sado River, has one foot in modern times and amenities and the other in old-school southern European charisma. Setúbal is home to notable historical monuments such as the Convent of Jesus, which represents the Manueline style of Portuguese late Gothic architecture. Other landmarks include the Church of São Julião with its Manueline portals.

Located to the south of Lisbon, Setúbal enjoys several geographical privileges. The city is nestled among the Arrábida Hills, embraced by both the Sado River and the Atlantic Ocean, sitting right in front of the stunning Tróia Peninsula. Over here, sandy beaches and clear waters abound.

If you also value having international schools, health care, and services in general, besides being close to the capital (and being able to get there in about an hour using public transportation), then Setúbal definitely deserves your attention.

The city center boasts the charm typical of so many small, old, sunny fishing villages all over the country. There are plenty of cafés and restaurants, many focusing on the local cuisine, which is strongly based on grilled fish and seafood.

If you'd like a sunny, relaxed town by the river, close to touristy spots (Azeitão, Sesimbra, and Tróia, to name a few), not far from Alentejo but with lower prices and far fewer tourists than Lisbon or the Algarve, then this might be the place for you.

*** *** ***

⊚ Silver Coast: The other Algarve

The Silver Coast (Costa de Prata in Portuguese) is a treasure trove of natural wonders, cultural attractions, and culinary delights. Stretching between the southern region of Porto and the northern part of Lisbon, this region offers a stunning coastal experience. Whether you're in search of pristine beaches, historic castles, nature reserves, or ancient villages, the Silver Coast has it all.

Although the Silver Coast is not as favored as the Algarve, it's starting to be on the radar of an increasing number of expats for its more calm and affordable experience. In fact, it's been referred to as a "cheaper, less warm version of the Algarve."

On the one hand, choosing the Silver Coast will mean being able to indulge in the "sun, sea, and sand" lifestyle at (still) affordable prices. It also means a very laid-back daily routine where sometimes it may feel like nothing happens. Those who choose to live here love the region precisely because of that… But is that something you're looking for and would be happy with?

On the other hand, Porto, Lisbon, and Coimbra are easy to reach either by car or public transportation, so major cultural or sporting events are never far away.

Southern Portugal

⊚ Cacela Velha: Town with a view

Cacela Velha, one of the prime beauty spots of the Algarve shore, is best visited during the off-season. At quieter times of the year, you'll find a sleepy, picturesque village with whitewashed houses, cobbled lanes, a 16th-century fortress, and a charming church perched above one of the most breathtaking viewpoints in southern Portugal—overlooking the shimmering blue waters and sandbars of the Ria Formosa Natural Park.

Life here moves at a wonderfully slow pace. Locals enjoy long lunches in tiny cafés that serve up freshly grilled fish and chilled vinho verde, while artists and writers seek inspiration in the serene setting and golden light. There's an understated sophistication to Cacela Velha—a favorite escape for those in-the-know—without any of the bustle of neighboring tourist hubs.

Access to the beach below is by foot at low tide or by boat, adding to the secluded feel. On weekends, families gather on terraces, and the air is filled with the scent of salt, jasmine, and seafood. The village's calm, unspoiled atmosphere makes it a haven for people seeking peace, nature, and authenticity.

It's the kind of place where time seems to stand still, and for many, that's exactly the point.

***

⊚ Culatra: The most remote living in Portugal

The island of Culatra, nestled within the Ria Formosa Natural Park, is one of the Algarve's hidden treasures. With no cars to disturb the peace, life here moves to the rhythm of the tides and sea breezes. The island is home to two traditional fishing villages—Culatra and Farol—where fishermen still mend their nets by hand and the daily catch defines the menu at every eatery.

A short ferry ride from Olhão, Culatra feels worlds away from mainland Portugal. Sandy lanes replace roads, and wheelbarrows or small carts are the only form of "transport." The atmosphere is delightfully rustic: barefoot children play in the sand, neighbors chat across doorsteps, and visitors fall into an easy daily routine of long swims, beachcombing, and sunset toasts with cold beer or vinho verde.

The beaches are stunning—wide, white, and blissfully uncrowded even in high season. Praia da Culatra stretches along the ocean side of the island, offering soft sands and crystal-clear waters perfect for swimming. On the lagoon side, the waters are calmer, ideal for paddleboarding or simply floating.

Despite its simplicity, Culatra has a strong sense of community and a growing reputation among artists, nature lovers, and eco-travelers. There's a raw charm here—electricity arrived only in the late 20th century, and life remains deeply connected to the sea.

You can live on Culatra Island… but it's a very unique, semi-off-grid lifestyle that's not for everyone. Accessible only by ferry, with no banks, medical care, school, spotty Wi-Fi and cell signal, and limited shopping… this is the kind of lifestyle that appeals to very few full-time, but can be the best recipe for a getaway. This is a place where you come not for luxury, but for authenticity.

****

⦿ Estói: Where Roman and Rococo live side by side

The village of Estói, about 6 miles from Olhão, is a picturesque little place with much to offer. The highlight is an 18th-century Rococo-style palace with French-influenced gardens. It is now the Algarve's one "palace hotel," part of the Small Luxury Hotels of the World. Non-residents are welcome to take a drink in the sumptuous lounge areas above the gardens, with views out to the sea.

Estói also has the Algarve's most important Roman remains—the ruins of Milreu—which include a once-luxurious villa that was occupied for nearly a millennium. Mosaic floors and crumbling columns provide a glimpse into the grandeur of Roman life.

Despite its grand architecture, Estói remains a quiet and slow-paced village with a traditional Algarve feel. Locals gather in small cafés lining the main square, and life revolves around festivals, food, and family. Weekly markets and *festas* still bring the community together, while a growing number of international residents are drawn to Estói's peaceful charm, making it a low-key favorite for those who want to live somewhere tranquil but culturally rich. It's a lifestyle of simple pleasures, historic beauty, and timeless rhythm.

****

⦿ Faro: National park neighbor

Faro has much to offer, from a medieval town center to a university, from excellent restaurants and cafés to live concerts. Soak up the atmosphere of a southern, sunny city, where you'll find storks nesting on the tops of churches, outdoor food markets with everything from Algarve honey to mangos, narrow cobbled alleyways, and anarchic street art.

The Old Town, within medieval walls, has a cathedral where you can climb up the tower for views over Faro, the coast, and nearby islands.

What makes Faro stand out, either as a home or as a travel destination, is the Ria Formosa natural park, an atmospheric stretch of coast which is one of Portugal's most important wetlands. It starts just west of Faro and stretches for nearly 40 miles, up to Cacela Velha at the eastern end.

***

⦿ Ferragudo: Quintessential Algarve

Ferragudo, located on the south coast of the western Algarve, is the village that many see as the most picturesque and charming in the Algarve.

It retains most of its historical ambiance with its traditional fishermen's cottages and narrow cobbled streets. It has a quaint, unspoiled village-feel to it that so many other locations in the Algarve have lost.

The small harbor and walkway are lined with popular fish restaurants. All roads lead to the main square of Praça Rainha Dona Leonor. This is a lively place with several cafés and restaurants. It's a brilliant spot to sit with a coffee and a pastel de nata pastry and watch the world go by.

Exploring Ferragudo's narrow and cobbled streets is probably the best way to enjoy this town. You walk past brightly painted traditional houses and wend your way to the top, where the church overlooks the river across to Portimão and Praia da Rocha marina.

***

⦿ Fuzeta: Fishing village with flair

A fishing village with white-sand beaches and a historic lifeboat station standing on stilts in the water, Fuzeta has long had its admirers. In

stores in the world and certainly the most emblematic in Portugal. It has been a huge inspiration for writers and artists from all over the world, including "Harry Potter" author J. K. Rowling, who was a regular guest while she lived in Porto. It was the famous wooden staircases of Lello that inspired her vision of the Hogwarts' stairs, and Porto University's student uniforms (which aren't very different from those worn by all Portuguese students) that inspired the long black coats of the Hogwarts's uniforms.

***

From queens to keepsakes: The north's finest filigree

Although nowadays you get filigree virtually anywhere in Portugal, it really comes from the north of Portugal and is an important part of the traditional wedding dresses from the northernmost Minho region. Filigree is the art of working delicate gold and silver threads, finely intertwined to form elaborate pieces. Entirely handmade, it requires an immense degree of patience and skill from goldsmiths. The most famous filigree design is the "Heart of Viana" pendant, which has its origins in a commission made by Queen Dona Maria I (1734-1816). If you're not in the market for a wedding dress, you can get filigree as earrings or brooches, too.

***

Most tangled treasure in the north

In Portugal, *bilros* lace is connected to the fishing areas of the coast, with written references from 1616 to *bilros* lace makers. *Bilros* is very delicate, with a variety of stitches and patterns that allow for a huge diversity of results.

To the women in fishing villages, *bilros* became a viable subsistence activity, especially when the men were away fishing or emigrated. Little towns like Póvoa de Varzim and Vila do Conde in the north, Peniche and Sesimbra on the central coast around Lisbon, and Lagos in the south have a strong tradition in this type of embroidery. You might find it in other places, including inland, but the tradition is strongest near the sea. Vila do Conde claims a special relationship with the art and even has an annual craft fair and museum dedicated to it, where you can watch artists weave and learn how to do it yourself. Watching an artisan making *bilros* lace is nothing short of mind-blowing!

stores in the world and certainly the most emblematic in Portugal. It has been a huge inspiration for writers and artists from all over the world, including "Harry Potter" author J. K. Rowling, who was a regular guest while she lived in Porto. It was the famous wooden staircases of Lello that inspired her vision of the Hogwarts' stairs, and Porto University's student uniforms (which aren't very different from those worn by all Portuguese students) that inspired the long black coats of the Hogwarts's uniforms.

***

From queens to keepsakes: The north's finest filigree

Although nowadays you get filigree virtually anywhere in Portugal, it really comes from the north of Portugal and is an important part of the traditional wedding dresses from the northernmost Minho region. Filigree is the art of working delicate gold and silver threads, finely intertwined to form elaborate pieces. Entirely handmade, it requires an immense degree of patience and skill from goldsmiths. The most famous filigree design is the "Heart of Viana" pendant, which has its origins in a commission made by Queen Dona Maria I (1734-1816). If you're not in the market for a wedding dress, you can get filigree as earrings or brooches, too.

***

Most tangled treasure in the north

In Portugal, *bilros* lace is connected to the fishing areas of the coast, with written references from 1616 to *bilros* lace makers. *Bilros* is very delicate, with a variety of stitches and patterns that allow for a huge diversity of results.

To the women in fishing villages, *bilros* became a viable subsistence activity, especially when the men were away fishing or emigrated. Little towns like Póvoa de Varzim and Vila do Conde in the north, Peniche and Sesimbra on the central coast around Lisbon, and Lagos in the south have a strong tradition in this type of embroidery. You might find it in other places, including inland, but the tradition is strongest near the sea. Vila do Conde claims a special relationship with the art and even has an annual craft fair and museum dedicated to it, where you can watch artists weave and learn how to do it yourself. Watching an artisan making *bilros* lace is nothing short of mind-blowing!

points for retirees and holidaymakers alike. You can lunch outdoors all year round.

If you love the sea and the lure of islands a short ferry ride away, Olhão could be just the place for you. It suits those who want to live in a town that isn't too big while also profiting from a more substantial settlement, the Algarve capital, Faro, right next door.

***

⊚ Parises: Mountain hamlet lost in time

Take the slow road to Parises, and you go back in time. This windy road, sometimes fringed by cork oaks, climbs steadily into remote, lonely country, the Serra do Caldeirão.

For centuries, the sparse population in these hills had comparatively little contact with outsiders, and you still pick up vibes of a place apart, a place where the Algarve coast is another world. Parises is a mountain hamlet with a few whitewashed houses, piles of cork lying by the roadside, and a little café, restaurant, and shop that could serve as a set for a Portuguese film set 50 years ago.

***

⊚ Silves: Step back in time

Silves is home to Roman ruins… a fantastic castle perched on the top of the hill, surrounded by beautiful countryside… A wealth of shops, activities, restaurants, and amenities… Tucked in a natural geographic basin that ensures amazing weather… All this, and it's only 20 minutes from several stunning Algarve beaches.

Silves is a fascinating historical delight and excellent place to make your new home. It's a popular vacation destination and a day tripper's paradise, but it has a different vibe to most of the beach resorts nearby. It's a proper town, where people live, work, commute, and socialize. It's home to a population of about 11,000, made up of many Portuguese and expats from across the world.

This is the real Algarve—before tourism captured and transformed so much of this area. Living here is like turning back the clock…

***

⦿ Tavira: Off the tourist tracks

Tavira is one of our favorite towns in Algarve and was named the #1 Retirement Haven in 2021. You'll love this town for its four-sided, double-sloped rooftops, tiled walls, Moorish-accented architecture, and impeccably groomed municipal gardens near Bishop's Square and the Fontaine aux Tortues. Tavira is known in Portugal for its great multitude of churches—there are more than 20 of them.

Living here is easygoing. Aside from the seaside, Tavira offers a wonderful countryside. Driving north, you enter the mountains with their beautiful green valleys and little villages…

Because there's no direct access to the nearby beaches, this is a place to come that doesn't feel overwhelmed in the high season. The beaches and lagoons are stunning… Great for walking and birdwatching. In the hinterland, there's space and wild areas. The air is clean, and of course, it's a golfer's paradise.

It's a historic town with enough rough edges to give it character and charm. And there's a sense of community here. It feels safe and makes you feel like you belong. You'll enjoy the clear blue skies, warmth, and sunshine. It's not too big, and it's not too small. It's just right.

Tavira is a river town, just a short ferry ride from the sea. The population of the municipality is about 28,000. Within minutes of driving out of town you pass through orange groves and up into gentle rolling hills.

Foreigners, often of retirement age, have arrived in considerable numbers to live here, with Swedes, Italians, French, Germans, British, and Irish all represented. According to local realtors, in recent years Americans and Canadians have started to feature in the international mix.

For thousands of years, the history of Tavira in particular and the Algarve in general was closely bound up with the tuna fish. According to the town's tourism literature, Tavira boasts the oldest tuna fishing net found anywhere in the world.

***

⦿ Vila da Luz: Light of the Algarve

Vila da Luz wraps itself around a picturesque sandy bay and was originally a small fishing village. It's located in the western Algarve, one hour west of Faro airport. Sandwiched between the towns of Lagos (about 4 miles) and Burgau (3 miles), it's ideally situated for exploring the region's best sights.

Luz's wow factor is the large sandy beach with its calm sea. Although—be warned—that water may look inviting, but it will probably be exhilaratingly cold. The main beach sits comfortably between the towering Rocha Negra headland on the east and the rocky coastline close to the Fortaleza da Luz.

You can also hike along the top of the cliffs and enjoy the magnificent, far-reaching views. The route is described as a challenging hiking trail, so wear something suitable on your feet.

A short walk beside the palm tree-lined promenade, which you could easily do in flip-flops, will take you to Prainha da Luz beach next to the fort. This is a small beach surrounded by rocks, favored by people looking for peace and quiet. The promenade walk itself is lovely, with patterns swirling in the design of the *calçadas* or pavement stones. The path overlooks the beach and is backed by shops, cafés, bars, and restaurants.

Praia da Luz has a year-round international community living in the town and local area. There are tennis clubs, various golf courses a short drive away, cycling and walking routes, dance groups, local centers to enjoy yoga and tai chi, plus great local areas for birdwatching and hiking.

***

⚲ Vila Real De Santo António: Italy in Portugal

Vila Real De Santo António (VRSA), a riverside haven on the Algarve's edge, is the easternmost town on Portugal's Algarve coast. Next door, on the other side of the Guadiana river, is Spain. The international flavor is strong. Spanish is often heard in the street, and ferries leave for the Spanish town of Ayamonte, a short ride upstream on the other side. Further upriver, but clearly visible from the town, an elegant modern road bridge links Portugal to its neighbor. The center of VRSA is slightly away from the river, the Praça Marquês de Pombal, named for the man who built the town. One side of the square is lined with restaurants, and there is usually plenty of street life. An obelisk stands in the center of the square, striking a note of municipal pride. To get the feel of the town, stroll along the Avenida da República, the promenade that follows the river. A line of tall palm trees and a marina with pleasure boats create a distinct atmosphere of Old World seaside holiday.

About 1,500 Italians live here for at least part of the year, according to one leading member of the Italian community, Enrico Venti. He said the numbers have grown considerably in recent years.

The splendid beach and the quietness are the key benefits expats cite about living here, as well as the fact that it's on the border. In a few minutes you can be in another culture with another rhythm of life.

You can't see the beach from town, but it's not far away—just a few minutes by car. Follow the river downstream on a rather bumpy, hard-surface road, and turn right onto a gravel track leading to Santo António beach. Stop when you see a boardwalk on your left. A five-minute walk, past low trees and flowers, takes you to a sandy beach that, at least in the off-season, is quiet. To your right, the beach sweeps on for as far as the eye can see.

VRSA should suit those who want the experience of living in a compact town, with shops and other amenities within walking distance. It also offers proximity to the sea and a certain international vibe, being next to Spain and with such a large population of Italians.

The Islands

⊙ Azores: Atlantic floating garden

The Azores is made up of nine volcanic islands scattered across the North Atlantic Ocean, about two hours' flight from Lisbon and is often compared to a blend of Hawaii, Iceland, and Ireland. These islands are known for their lush landscapes, dramatic cliffs, crater lakes, volcanic hot springs, and charming small towns.

Life in the Azores is slow, peaceful, and deeply connected to nature. It's ideal for those who value a laid-back, community-oriented lifestyle over the fast pace of big cities. There's very little traffic, low crime, and a genuine friendliness among locals. People greet each other on the street, and time is less rigid—things move at an island rhythm.

While the Azores are remote, they have good infrastructure, especially on São Miguel and Terceira. You'll find hospitals, schools, supermarkets, and fiber-optic internet in most towns. Inter-island flights and ferries make it possible to travel between islands, though this can sometimes be weather-dependent.

The climate here is very humid, though, it's geographically isolated, and options are limited when it comes to shopping.

If you love nature, peace, and community, the Azores can be paradise. But be prepared for the trade-offs in convenience, accessibility, and modern amenities. Many expats and remote workers thrive here—but only after adjusting expectations.

***

⊙ **Madeira:** Hawaii of Europe

Madeira: It's Europe… but tropical. Madeira is an archipelago made up of three main islands (Madeira, Porto Santo, and the Desertas) that float about 620 miles southwest of mainland Europe in the North Atlantic Ocean. Madeira is geographically closer to Africa (the coast of Morocco is only 320 miles away) and on the same parallel as Bermuda.

A giant chunk of seafloor wrenched above the surface, Madeira has a dramatic landscape full of jagged peaks and wind-sculpted cliffs. Sweeping sea views are available from most vantage points.

Lush vegetation abounds, including wild pineapple, banana, and passionfruit. Again, not what you expect from Europe… In fact, Hawaii was the first place that came to mind. Bali was the second.

It's only when you get to the Old Town of Funchal and see the narrow cobblestone streets, historical buildings, and thriving café culture that you're reminded that you are indeed in the Old World. Culturally and politically, Madeira is very much part of Portugal, but it stands out from the mainland (in more ways than just its geography).

Madeira is in a unique climate zone. It's called the island of eternal spring because of its pleasant year-round weather, which includes warm ocean waters. Its tourism industry is year-round, unaffected by the seasons.

Madeira's motto is "Of all islands, the most beautiful and free." It's also known as "Garden Island" for its abundance of verdant vegetation and exotic plants that contrast against the blue Atlantic it's surrounded by.

Madeira has been voted the best island in the world several times. Its beaches are award-winning, too. All around Madeira are natural pools that fill and empty with the changing tides. The island is laced by ancient irrigation lines called *levadas*, which are today popular hiking routes. It has unique geographic features like capes, canyons, and caves. Golf, surfing, big game fishing, birdwatching, kayaking, sailing, scuba diving, and whale-watching are a few of the things you can do here. There's also an active culture and gastronomy scene that includes seafood and its eponymous libation, Madeira wine.

Madeira has a hearty, healthy, well-established expat community. It numbers about 10,000, and about 10% of those are Brits. Germans are the next-biggest demographic.

There are two expat communities in Madeira: the traditional one, mainly made up of older Brits and Germans who have been here for decades, and the digital nomad one, which hails from all over the world and is a newer group.

Madeira's chief appeal is its natural beauty, and with this, plus a near-perfect climate, comes a variety of outdoor activities you can enjoy.

It's surrounded by ocean, so naturally, many activities involve the sea, from boating, sailing, big game fishing, whale-watching, surfing, diving, and more.

All around the island are natural swimming pools that have been carved out of the volcanic rock. They fill and empty with the tides and are a perfect place to go for a peaceful dip. Because of the Gulf Stream, the ocean waters around Madeira are always warm.

If you're a beach lover, you'll be happy to know that several of its beaches have won accolades for their outstanding beauty. Porto Santo Beach (on Porto Santo Island) is beloved by locals for its sandy shores. Seixal Beach (Madeira) is another favorite.

On land, hiking is a popular pastime. The islands were formed by volcanic activity and feature many points of elevation, so spectacular scenery is a given.

Life close to the sea with stunning ocean vistas… dramatic green landscapes sheathed in flowers, where tropical fruits grow naturally… perpetual spring-like weather… and strong tourism, with the potential for year-round rental income and steady appreciation in property values.

This is a quiet, peaceful place that's full of natural beauty and unique appeal. If living on a tiny island doesn't daunt you, you owe it to yourself to check out what Madeira has to offer.

2. Residency Programs

The easiest visa option for retirees

There is no specific visa for retirees in Portugal, but the D7 visa is what most retirees use to seek permanent residency, and it's arguably the easiest and most affordable visa available in Europe.

To qualify, you need to prove you receive a mere 1,200 euros per month in passive income, and you need to commit to spending 180 days per year in the country. The visa is valid for two years initially and can be renewed for an additional three years.

You must apply through the Portuguese embassy or consulate in your home country before arriving. Once in Portugal, the next step is applying for a residence permit ("Autorização de Residência") through AIMA, Agência para a Integração, Migrações e Asilo (https://aima.gov.pt/pt).

***

The most important 9 digits you have here

The NIF (Número de Identificação Fiscal) is vital for virtually any financial activity in Portugal. You'll need it to open a bank account, rent a house, pay taxes, or sign up for utilities. Even the cashier at your local supermarket will ask you if you'd like your invoice with your NIF.

You can obtain your NIF from a local tax office, the Serviço de Finanças, either in person or through a representative if you're not in the country yet.

The sooner you have it, the easier setting up your life in Portugal will be.

3. Social And Senior Programs

Seniors skip the line

A 2016 law requires all public and private entities to provide priority services to people over the age of 65, as well as to the physically challenged, pregnant women, anyone holding or escorting children under 2 years old, and people with physical and/or mental disabilities.

The public, including visitors to the country, must—by law—give away their first-come, first-served privilege when waiting at customer services in public and private venues, such as:

- ❖ Hospitals
- ❖ Supermarkets
- ❖ Banks
- ❖ Pharmacies
- ❖ Airports
- ❖ Public transportation
- ❖ And other similar settings

And the law is enforced. People or institutions that don't comply will receive a social misconduct offense, punishable by a fine of 50 to 500 euros for individuals and 100 to 1,000 euros for institutions.

*****

Door-to-door doctor service

Porto city hall launched a service aimed at the elderly population, called Táxi Saúde +65. This allows citizens who are 65 and older to take a taxi to any health care facility, public or private, 24/7, within the city of Porto, paying only 2 euros for each ride. A trip to the local Centro de Saúde, for example, is only a phone call away and will cost a total of 4 euros.

*****

Accessibility Regulations

The Portuguese have an informal approach to regulations relating to disability. You won't find disabled-friendly restaurants listed, for instance, but you will find staff willing to accommodate you and assist you in any way that they can.

Most public buildings have a disabled access, and all major parking lots and shopping centers have designated disabled parking spaces.

Older buildings tend not to have elevators. If you have limited mobility, be extra careful when looking for properties.

It takes a village

Portuguese communities provide programs for seniors at schools, libraries, plazas, churches, or civic centers. Some of the activities for folks over 65 include crafts, book clubs, musical performances, tours of local venues like museums and zoos, chair yoga and exercise classes, cooking demos, bird watching, and presentations by guest speakers. Intergenerational activities are available as well.

And they're all typically free.

***

All-age holidays

All age groups make processions through the streets in traditional dress to open municipal festivals at Easter, Christmas, or the day celebrating the city's patron saint. Senior organizations spend many hours of preparation, with all age groups helping to create costumes and banners. This is just one way that elders organize and pass down the traditions with the support of their children, grandchildren, and civic employees.

***

Free education for the elderly

The University of the Third Age (Associação Rede de Universidades da Terceira Idade) provides classes specifically for people over the age of 50 at campuses throughout Portugal. These classes are free. And if you incur costs traveling to the classes, those expenses are reimbursed.

***

Savings for seniors

Portugal offers many senior discounts—not just at the movie theater but also on monthly bus and metro transit passes, train tickets throughout the country, concerts, and restaurants, to name a few.

***

4. Health Care

How to get the health care

To access public health care services in Portugal, you'll need to register with the Serviço Nacional de Saúde (SNS) at your local health center (Centro de Saúde). This requires your passport, residence permit, and social security number.

Upon securing legal residency of any kind (even the digital nomad visa), everyone gains the right to use the public health care services, which are known for their excellence and affordability.

If you are not yet retired, and are working or studying in Portugal, this step will also require your NISS, Número de Identificação da Segurança Social, which can be requested at your local Social Security department.

In the case of EU citizens, having a European Health Insurance Card (EHIC) can help cover initial health care needs while you get settled, but you'll eventually need to register with the SNS for long-term access. Alternatively, you may choose to arrange private health insurance, which can offer quicker access to some medical services.

The SNS provides access to a wide range of medical services at little to no cost, covering things like general practitioner visits, routine exams, hospital care, maternity services, and some prescription medications.

***

Public Versus Private

In Europe, health care is seen as a fundamental right, not a privilege, and no one is denied care based on income. But any system that serves so many faces challenges of availability.

The public health care here is high-quality, but it can have long waiting times for non-emergency procedures and a shortage of medical professionals in certain regions.

Because of this, most locals and expats also have private health insurance and opt for a mix of public and private care. For example, go to an SNS general practitioner for basic bloodwork, but go to a private clinic for an eye checkup.

Digitize your care

SNS 24 is a direct connection via website or the app to your public health care profile and those in your family. You can check your vaccination status, call the 24-hour hotline, get prescriptions, schedule appointments and exams, do teleconsultations, save and access documents and certificates, monitor your ongoing health, and more.

***

A healthy track record

There are programs for preventive health care and home visits to support living independently through the national health care system.

During the pandemic, these programs, which were also supported by the country's military, were amped up. People of an advanced age did not go to vaccination centers. Teams in hazmat suits came to their homes to deliver vaccines.

Groceries were distributed, too, at no cost to the recipient. It yielded the highest vaccination rate in the EU and delivered one of the lowest percentages of mortality worldwide.

This is indicative of the level of care you can expect in Portugal through the national system, even in a worst case scenario—and it's notable that seniors are prioritized in any health care situation.

***

Insurance specialists

The Association for Foreign Residents and Visitors (AFPOP) group charges an annual membership of 85 euros (or 100 euros for a couple), which entitles you to discounted health insurance policies as well as many other services and activities, in addition to providing information and personalized consultation.

***

5. Community

Expat Networks

The rotary realm

One way to get involved in the local community is to join the nearest Rotary Club chapter. Rotary is an international, English-speaking organization that regularly hosts charity events and fundraisers. They support charities and the local community as well as supporting Rotary International activities around the world. There are over 130 chapters operating throughout Portugal, so it's easy to find one no matter where you settle.

***

Best for business

InterNations, a global expat networking group, exists here as it does in many countries. It's often better for business connections than personal ones, though each specific chapter will vary. Many expats love it for the forums where they can ask questions and get referrals from current expats.

***

Facebook fundamentals

As a starting point, Facebook should be at the top of your list for finding friends in your new home. All sorts of groups and clubs meet across the country, and Facebook is an excellent place to look for them. There are sports clubs and activities for all ages and abilities, as well as art and photography classes and groups.

Just type in "expats in X" (X being your town or village), and get more specific from there with variations like "English-speaking expats," "retired expats," "expat gardening," expat yoga"… etc., etc. Join them all and get active in the space. Once you find the most useful groups, you can get answers to questions about everything from yoga classes to good plumbers. Exchange opinions with and get advice from fellow expats… just make sure to keep in mind that the internet can be an echo chamber for grumblers who like some company with their complaints.

***

Run and fun

The famous international running group, Hash House Harriers, has several chapters throughout the country, including in Algarve, Lisbon, and Porto. With the motto "A drinking club with a running problem," you know this is a good way to meet fellow runners and fitness enthusiasts who still know how to have fun!

***

Acclimate with activities

The Facebook group Algarve Active Life is an English-speaking group that brings together fitness enthusiasts in the region for walking, hiking, running, buking, pickleball, padel, and more.

***

Big-picture assistance

ExpatExchange.com helps newcomers get their bearings in a new country, and it has one forum devoted exclusively to the Algarve.

***

Prepping for Portugal

Since 2005, Expats Portugal has helped thousands of people move to Portugal and live in Portugal successfully through advice, resources, and knowledge. Discover life in Portugal by joining their community of over 15,000 members today.

***

Friends through Fido

Having a dog that requires a couple of nice long walks every day is an excellent way to meet people, especially locals. You'll become recognized in your neighborhood, thanks to your pup, and the more you get out and explore, the more fun places you'll find to spend time. Plus, you're likely to see other groups of dog owners out walking or playing in parks, and they may have a regular schedule or a text group that you can plug into.

***

Resource for the un-retired

Worktugal is a remote work hub with over 19,000 members of remote professionals, founders, and freelancers. They can help with moving, legal set up, and growing your network.

***

Queer Connections

Portugal is often said to be one of the most LGBTQ+ friendly countries in Europe. Legislation passed in recent years backs this up. In 2010, Portugal was one of the first European countries to legalize same-sex marriage. The right to marry was added to the Portuguese constitution. The Law of Gender Identity followed right after in 2011, and the right to adoption by same-sex couples was legalized in 2016.

Accepting and welcoming as Portugal is, keep in mind that gay culture here is often more conservative and low-key than what you might be used to back home, depending on where you're from.

***

Finding your tribe

There are gay clubs, shops, bars, and restaurants in bigger Portuguese cities. Be sure to check out the Portuguese gay groups and blogs on social media sites. Businesses catering specifically to LGBTQ+ clientele don't exist as you move away from the large city centers, but that doesn't mean there is no gay community outside the big cities. You might not find an online presence in smaller towns or in the countryside, and although it may be slower in coming, you're very likely to find a gay community anywhere in the country. But rest assured, queer friends aside, you'll be welcomed by your new home as a whole.

***

Love is love in Lisbon

Lisbon is one of the most LGBTQ+ friendly cities in Europe and the world. Besides LGBTQ+ friendly bars and clubs, Lisbon hosts several events, like Queer Lisboa - Lisbon Gay & Lesbian Film Festival and the

Arraial Lisbon Pride, an outdoor celebration that takes place every year in Terreiro do Paço, attracting thousands of people.

***

Special Silver Coast spots

Some favorite gay-friendly bars in the Silver Coast region include Glitz Club in Leiria and Angel's Bar in Coimbra.

***

Pride in Porto

Although the LGBTQ+ community in Porto is not as busy as in Lisbon, there's a lot going on, especially in terms of nightlife. Some places have become well known spots of the local LGBTQ+ scene, like the Pride Coffee bar. Queer saunas are also a thing, like Sauna Thermas 205 and Sauna Camões, for example. Throughout the year, there are small events taking place, but the yearly Porto Pride is the most significant LGBTQ+ celebration in the north of the country, attracting thousands of people.

***

Socializing on the southern coast

Albufeira is the hub for the Algarve's gay club scene, with smaller clubs in Portimão and Lagos.

***

Primo Central Portugal parade

Aveiro has a Pride Parade in June (Marcha do Orgulho LGBTQ+ de Aveiro) that's a favorite within the region.

6. Real Estate

Finding a home on a foreign continent with a foreign currency, language, culture, traditions, and real estate market is daunting.

It's all a world you don't know. You need to seek on-the-ground help to avoid pitfalls.

However, to get acquainted with things, here's a quick cheat sheet of some of the big differences you need to be aware of.

A Pocket Guide To Local Real Estate Jargon

Portugal has a range of property types available, including multi-purpose and multiple dwelling structures, store-top flats, residential condominiums, resort apartments, and more…

But how to identify them according to their local names? Here are some common terms to start you off…

* ❖ **Algarvean Cottage:** Refers to the traditional architectural style of this region (typically measuring about 120 square meters).

* ❖ ***Alojamento Local (AL):*** Also called *arrendamento de curta duração*, this is a short-term rental, from a few nights to a few months. *Alojamento local* is a regulated designation for short-term rentals to tourists. Properties must be registered with the local municipality.

* ❖ ***Arrendamento de média duração:*** Also called *renda mensal flexível* or "flexible monthly rental," this is a rental from 1 to 12 months.

* ❖ ***Arrendamento de longa duração:*** Often just referred to as *arrendamento*, this is a rental of at least one year. Typically unfurnished or semi-furnished, these are regulated by Portuguese tenancy law (NRAU – *Novo Regime do Arrendamento Urbano*).

* ❖ ***Andar:*** Floor level (1st, 2nd, etc.), but keep in mind the first floor in Portugal is the one above the ground floor (R/C).

* ❖ ***Área bruta / área útil:*** *Área bruta* is gross area (including walls, balconies, etc.); *área útil* is usable living area (inside walls only).

- ❖ ***Arrecadação:*** Storage room, often in the basement or attic.

- ❖ ***Atualizações necessárias:*** Needs updates.

- ❖ ***À venda / vende-se:*** For sale; you'll see these types of properties for sale: *Imóvel* is a building, *casa* is a house, *apartamento* is an apartment, and *terreno* is land.

- ❖ ***Casa para reabilitar:*** House to rehabilitate, often used with older homes.

- ❖ ***Condomínio:*** The building's shared ownership structure. Also refers to the monthly fee paid for maintenance of common areas.

- ❖ ***Cozinha equipada:*** Equipped kitchen, includes appliances.

- ❖ ***Cozinha mobilada:*** Furnished kitchen, includes cabinets but not necessarily appliances.

- ❖ ***Elevador:*** Elevator—important to check, especially in older buildings.

- ❖ ***Frente:*** Street-facing.

- ❖ ***Habitação em ruínas:*** Home in ruins—heavy fixer-upper or tear-down.

- ❖ ***Habitação permanente / Habitação secundária:*** Indicates whether the property is for full-time living or a second/vacation home. This affects taxes and utility rates.

- ❖ ***Imóvel para recuperar:*** Property to recover/restore.

- ❖ ***Logradouro:*** Outdoor space or yard, typically private to the unit or house.

- ❖ ***Lugar de garagem / Box:*** Parking space (open or closed box garage).

❖ *Marquise:* An enclosed balcony or veranda, often with windows—used like a sunroom.

❖ *Moradia:* A detached or semi-detached house (single-family home). A *moradia geminada* is semi-detached; *moradia isolada* is fully detached; *moradia em banda* is a row house.

❖ *Obra total:* Total renovation (gut job).

❖ *Para demolição:* To be demolished (tear down job).

❖ *Pequenas obras:* Small works needed.

❖ *Prédio:* A building (usually apartment block).

❖ *Precisa de obras:* Needs renovation (literally "needs works"); this is the most common phrase you'll see in listings. *Para renovar* means to renovate.

❖ *Precisa de remodelação complete:* Needs complete remodeling (gut job).

❖ *Quinta:* You may see the word *quinta*, which refers to a home on rural acreage or any property built on former farmland. (A *rancho*, which is the Spanish word for this type of property, actually means a troupe of dancers in Portuguese.)

❖ *R/C (Rés-do-chão):* Ground floor.

❖ *Reabilitação integral:* Full rehabilitation (gut job).

❖ *Reconstrução necessária:* Reconstruction needed (gut job).

❖ *Remodelado parcialmente:* Partially remodeled.

❖ *T's:* Portuguese real estate listings will use terms like T1 or T2 to describe the size of the property. The "T" represents the number of bedrooms. (So, a T0 is a studio, a T1 is a one bedroom, a T2 is a two bedroom, and so on.)

❖ ***Urbanization:*** Pre-planned neighborhoods of new-build town-houses, villas, and apartments found on the outskirts of most towns. They look a lot like North American sub-divisions—somewhat cookie-cutter and not as architecturally unique as the historic homes.

But they're built on new, wide roads, have less traffic and more parking… on the other hand, these aren't neighborhoods in the sense a village is—there are no bakeries, shops, markets, etc., to walk to. *Urbanization* units usually offer more spacious rooms, built-in heating and air conditioning, elevators, extra amenities, and larger and more modern kitchens and bathrooms. They feel familiar and meet modern convenience standards.

The quality of municipally funded maintenance in *urbanization* is also impressive. Street-cleaning cars and crews of gardeners typically come to these neighborhoods weekly. Common areas are planted with flowers, bushes, and trees and are weeded and groomed.

These buildings will usually have a security system, triple-locked heavy unit doors, a closed-in underground garage, and electric metal blinds on the outside of every window, which provide great shade in the summer, and all of these features combine for an easy lock-up-and-leave scenario.

❖ ***Villa:*** is any detached, semi-detached, or townhouse that has a yard or urban land around it.

❖ ***Vista mar / vista rio:*** Sea view / river view.

❖ ***Vivenda:*** Another term for a house or villa—used interchangeably with *moradia*, but often implies a standalone, detached home.

Administrative Basics

Paperwork, permits, the shortage of available contractors, historical façade preservation rules, antiquated plumbing and electrical systems, and issues with adjoining buildings are major hurdles to have to jump over.

Don't be ignorant of the basics…

***

Rental realities

There are three types of official rental methods in Portugal:

❖ **Rentals with AL licenses that are still in operation.** The rental for short-term holidays is the most common for an AL license. It is booked and paid by the day or duration of the stay, (up to a limit of 30 days).

❖ **Short-term rentals, or "rentals for non-permanent habitation,"** require proper contracts stating the rental periods (permitted once a year, from 30 days up to 12 months). These must also state the purpose of use—work, tourism, studies, student accommodations, and so on. These are not AL license rentals; these are normal and binding rental contracts, paid monthly.

❖ **Long-term rentals, or "rentals for habitation."** These are for longer periods of time, from one year to a maximum of 30 years. The purpose of use must be residency. Payments are made monthly, and legal contracts are mandatory.

***

Legal obligations

Lawyers are mandatory for property purchases, and Portuguese law states that foreign buyers must have a fiscal number (the NIF, similar to a Social Security number) and a registered fiscal representative. Having a strong legal team in place is an important final piece of the property asset process.

A qualified English-speaking attorney can set you up with a NIF number and help handle the purchase of your new home. They can also arrange home insurance, electric, gas, and water utility accounts. This service can be included in the property purchase fee and listed in the closing costs (which will be less than anything you'd pay in the U.S.)

***

Budgeting for the bureaucracy

Stamp Duty, Municipal Real Estate Transfer Tax (IMT), Deed, and Registry charges will be assessed on your final documents, but no funds will be directed to your real estate agent, who is paid in full by the seller.

Expect to pay 7% to 8% in closing costs, including lawyer's fees. This does not include costs associated with a mortgage.

***

Resident benefit

Portuguese residents incorporate profit resulting from property sales into their annual income tax filing. They usually pay tax on half the total, based on their tax rate in the year their property was sold.

For non-residents, closing costs absorb almost one-third of profits (generally around 28%) realized from real estate sales.

***

Resident rates

As a resident of Portugal, if you sell property anywhere in the world, 50% of the gain is added to your annual income and taxed at the relevant rate. You can avoid this, however, if you reinvest the proceeds in a new home in Portugal or elsewhere in the EU.

7. Utilities And Service Providers

Infrastructure is generally reliable throughout the country, but the more rural you go, the more your options will be reduced and perhaps also the quality.

Compared to the United States, though, it's all highly affordable. A basic phone package , for example, will cost you about 20 euros a month and an internet and TV package, about 35 euros a month.

When it comes to finding a helping hand for hire, for any service you'd like, be it plumber, handyman, doctor or lawyer… the best way to find someone is through referrals. Ask around, confer with other expats, ask in online forums, ask at the corner shop, ask neighbors, etc.

Hot hookups

There are three main broadband providers in Portugal, each with their own dedicated networks. MEO, NOS, and Vodafone all provide internet, television, and mobile services.

***

Iffy internet?

Data speed and availability can depend greatly on location. The worst option is 3G, which can be extremely slow (3 to 4 Mbps), and even worse in the peak of the summer months, when usage outstrips availability. The best option is fiber-optic broadband with unlimited downloads and speeds of about 100 Mbps. Make sure to check this wherever you settle in the country to be sure that your internet needs will be met.

***

Help getting help

The best way to find a cleaner is to ask around for people who are available and trustworthy. Small local shops and neighbors are good options to try this. The local expat Facebook groups are a great place to start your search. In the Lisbon area, the hourly price for a cleaner starts at 7 euros, with the final price depending on how physically demanding the work is going to be.

* * *

Care for the kids

Babysitters and nannies aren't as easy to find as they are in other countries. Expat moms find the best candidates are their kids' teachers. It's worth asking around your kids' school if any of the teachers like to babysit to make extra money in the evenings and on weekends.

The Best Of Portugal
For The Global Citizen

Portugal has become one of Europe's most attractive destinations for those seeking not just a beautiful place to live, but also a smart hub for long-term investment.

In this section, we'll explore the key pathways available—from residency and citizenship options to favorable tax regimes, banking advantages, business opportunities, and investor incentives.

These opportunities stand out as some of the most compelling programs anywhere in Europe, making Portugal a top choice for globally minded individuals...

1. Residency Options

Easiest option for the self-sufficient

The best residency-by-income option in Portugal is the D7 visa, which is also the fastest route to residency. To qualify, you need to prove you receive a mere 1,200 euros per month in passive income, and you need to commit to spending 180 days per year in the country. The visa is valid for two years initially and can be renewed for an additional three years.

***

Best path for the remote workforce

The best way to stay in Portugal as a remote worker is through the digital nomad visa.

For this one, you'll need to show that you earn 3,040 euros per month, which is a major difference between the D7 and D8 visas: the income requirement is higher. It reflects the expected financial stability of its applicants—and that they will contribute to the local economy.

The interesting thing about Portugal's digital nomad visa, as opposed to those of most other countries, is that it actually offers a path to long-term residency, which can seamlessly lead to permanent residency or citizenship.

It's also possible to just take it as a short-term residency option, renewable yearly, ideal for those exploring Portugal as a temporary base.

This dual approach caters to a broad spectrum of digital nomads, from those seeking a brief change of scenery to others looking to lay down roots in Portugal.

The straightforward process for transitioning from a temporary stay to a more permanent status underscores Portugal's desire to be more than just a stopover for digital nomads—it aims to be a place they can call home.

***

Best route for the entrepreneur

The D2 Entrepreneur Visa is the best option for a small business owner. You could either be an entrepreneur establishing a business in Portugal, have an existing business in your home country and establishing a branch in Portugal, or be self-employed intending to work in Portugal with a pre-existing work contract or a documented work proposal. Freelancers and digital nomads are also eligible if they can meet another set of criteria.

This permit is renewable every two years and allows you to bring family with you. After five years you can apply for citizenship (as of the July 2025 rules).

****

Change On The Horizon

The rules in Portugal have always allowed a resident to apply for citizenship after five years… but that's currently changing.

The proposed bill would require 7 or 10 years for citizenship via residency.

The real discussion now is who is or will be grandfathered in due to constitutional law constraints. Hopefully those who have already been living in Portugal will be allowed to follow the rules they came in on, but the debate is ongoing.

The bill discussion and approval were postponed to (at least) September 2025.

2. Citizenship Programs

Budget-friendly citizenship

The best way to gain Portuguese citizenship if you don't want to pay for it—and you have and want to spend the time in Portugal—is through naturalization. After five years of permanent residency on your D7 visa you can apply for citizenship.

*****

A golden opportunity

If you've got the budget for it, citizenship is also available through the Golden Visa program in exchange for a five-year investment in the country.

It will also take five years to acquire, but you don't have to be resident in Portugal to be eligible—meaning you also won't be tax resident during those years. As long as you visit the country for 14 days every two years, you'll remain compliant with the rules, and once the five years is up, you can apply for citizenship. Even better: the clock on those five years starts ticking when you submit your application, not when your residency card is actually issued.

You also have to pass a language test to show an A2 (pre-intermediate) level proficiency in Portuguese.

Golden Visa holders can live, work, and study in Portugal. If you choose to live in Portugal full-time, you will have access to public services like health care and education, but you'll also be on the hook for taxes.

Investment options include:

❖ **Venture Capital/Private Equity Fund:** Transferring at least 500,000 euros to acquire units in venture capital funds, as long as they are not connected to real estate. This amount can be distributed among multiple funds.

This is the most popular choice, as the funds offer a wide range of investment options and do not require active management or a donation to the government. Qualifying funds with incentives, such as fixed returns and upfront interest payments, are gaining quick interest.

❖ **Cultural Heritage Support:** Donating 250,000 euros or more to support arts or cultural heritage. If funding a qualifying initiative in a low-density region, this amount can be reduced to 200,000 euros.

❖ **Company Creation:** Creating a company or adding to the share capital of an already existing one, employing at least 10 locals (or 8, if done in a low-density area) alongside a capital transfer of 500,000 euros. If you are a business owner or entrepreneur in your home country, this option will let you build a European operation.

❖ **Donation to Research Activities:** Transferring at least 500,000 euros for research done by either public or private scientific research institutions.

3. Banking And Doing Business

Control the rates

The best way to mitigate the loss you might experience when it comes to exchanging from your home currency to euros is to have a local account as well as an exchange account with a company like MoneyCorp or Wise. With these components in place, you can easily move to convert funds when there's an attractive rate, instead of being at the mercy of bank wire fees and volatile exchange rates. Most Portuguese banks charge a monthly fee of between 5 and 10 euros for a basic account.

***

Cash is king

You never want to go out without some cash here, especially if you stop in a smaller restaurant or café, and many establishments do not have a card machine. It pays to ask before you sit down to eat if a card is all you've got. Larger stores will often take a visa card but not American Express.

***

ATM MVP

Multibanco cash machines here do much more than just give out cash. You can pay bills online, transfer money to other accounts or even your own PayPal account, buy tickets for concerts, shows, and the cinema, deposit cash, and even top up your mobile phone.

You can withdraw up to 400 euros a day from a Multibanco machine, which you'll find all over the country. Beware of the Euronet ones—they charge a fee for each withdrawal. Go to one of the machines that are actually linked to a bank instead.

***

Bankers' hours

Most banks open at 8:30 a.m. but close at 3 p.m. Some have an hour for lunch when they are closed too. Unless you are in a big city and are lucky, you will find all the banks are closed on the weekend.

✱

Need a bean counter

If you want to set up and run a business here, then an efficient accountant is worth their weight in gold. The system, to an outsider, can seem complicated, but with good supportive advice, once you are up and running, things can run successfully, although maybe more slowly than you're used to.

✱

4. Investor Incentives

The best incentive Portugal offers for investment is residency through its Golden Visa program.

5. Taxes At A Glance

Portugal no longer offers any special tax programs for foreign residents. On the other hand, it is one of the less onerous tax systems in Europe…

- ❖ **Income Tax:** 13.5% to 48%
- ❖ **Property Tax:** 0.3% to 0.8%
- ❖ **Capital Gains Tax:** 28%
- ❖ **Inheritance and Estate Taxes:** 10%
- ❖ **Tax treaty with the U.S.?** Yes
- ❖ **Tax treaty with Canada?** Yes

Would You Like To Stay In Touch With Kat?

Follow Her Adventures In Europe Here...

The world's savviest, most experienced, and most trusted source for information on living, retiring, and investing in Europe

Live And Invest Overseas is the most trusted name for finding opportunities for profit, fun, and better living abroad. Now Kat Kalashian is sharing our far-flung network's decades of experience living, traveling, investing, doing business, making money, and having a grand adventure in Europe. She shares her ongoing experiences around the world both through the www.liveandinvestoverseas.com website... and also through email. Kat's *In Focus: Europe* is a weekly dispatch from her, with contributions from our far-flung network of editors, experts, friends, and advisors. Each week you'll find out about the best opportunities for living, retiring, and investing in real estate in Europe.

In Focus: Europe is a completely free service. You can find out more at https://bit.ly/infoseurope

Made in the USA
Las Vegas, NV
08 October 2025

29264755R00163